PitmanScript Skill Book 3

100 Examination Passages
in Advanced PitmanScript
selected and edited by

Emily D. Smith
B.Sc.Econ. (Hons.), F.R.S.A.

Pitman Publishing

First published 1973

SIR ISAAC PITMAN AND SONS LTD.
Pitman House, Parker Street, Kingsway, London WC2B 5PB
P.O. Box 46038, Portal Street, Nairobi, Kenya
SIR ISAAC PITMAN (AUST.) PTY. LTD.
Pitman House, Bouverie Street, Carlton, Victoria 3053, Australia
PITMAN PUBLISHING COMPANY S.A. LTD.
P.O. Box 11231, Johannesburg, South Africa
PITMAN PUBLISHING CORPORATION
6 East 43rd Street, New York, N.Y. 10017, U.S.A.
SIR ISAAC PITMAN (CANADA) LTD.
495 Wellington Street West, Toronto 135, Canada
THE COPP CLARK PUBLISHING COMPANY
517 Wellington Street West, Toronto 135, Canada

ISBN: 0 273 00214 7

Reproduced and printed by photolithography and bound in Great Britain at The Pitman Press, Bath

G3 (S.5670:25)

PREFACE

A major premise of PITMANSCRIPT is that each and every writer, having mastered the fundamental characters and principles, is free to write as much or as little as is necessary to meet his own requirements. Provided that there is no misuse of the special consonants or special signs, the scriptor is free to manipulate the system in the way that brings him the most delight and profit.

That there is room for variety in PITMANSCRIPT is amply demonstrated in the writing that is contained in this book. There are one hundred passages, each a Public Examination speed test, which were first published for dictation practice under the title *Skill Book 2.* In the latter book each test is accompanied by a panel of suggested PITMANSCRIPT forms which are considered appropriate to a writer just beginning a course of speed training. With experience and increased knowledge, ability to abbreviate grows – and *Skill Book 3* is an attempt to show what PITMANSCRIPT can become in the hands of an advanced writer. Here, for instance, are examples of the type of link you can expect to find in these passages:

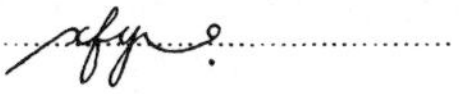 next few years

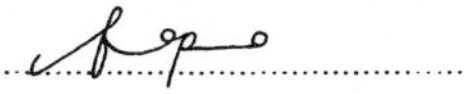 in the first place

 purpose of this letter

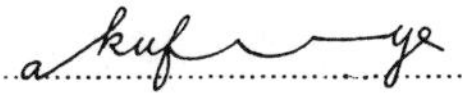 thank you for your letter of yesterday

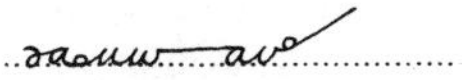 and as you will have seen

 we must expect a

 I have not been able to visit

The purpose of such links and of the other abbreviations used in the following passages is to help the scriptor to develop his ability to write the system quickly while retaining legibility. The factor of legibility can never be sacrificed, because notes which are partially illegible are useless — still worse, they are dangerous.

While in some forms of reporting an approximation to what was actually said may be acceptable, for examination and office purposes exactness is required. Therefore, any suggestions for speed development must be made with legibility in mind.

Links of the kind shown above help speed without sacrificing legibility, and it is unlikely that any reader will experience difficulty in transcribing the PITMANSCRIPT used in the pages which follow — in spite of the fact that it is much more refined than the style used in the *Basic Text.*

It could well be asked: why teach the longer forms if we are afterwards going to cut them down? There are very good reasons. In the first place, we cannot run before we can walk, and students of PITMANSCRIPT must first learn to recognize the sounds of words and interpret them correctly. They must also learn to recognize what they have written and to read it back accurately.

For a beginner a generous use of vowels is necessary, as the mind has not yet been trained to read by consonants alone: that is a skill which comes with practice. As experience grows, vowels become less and less important because the writers are becoming accustomed to reading words in relation to context and to knowing what makes good sense and what does not. Most of us have developed this ability when reading the "small ads" in newspapers and magazines, but we do not necessarily automatically transfer the ability to the reading of our notes — mainly because there is so much more variety in the matter with which we are working.

When scriptors have acquired an instant use of all the signs of PITMANSCRIPT and an ability to read their own notes with ease, they are ready to move on to the advanced stage. Their notes will contain fewer and fewer vowels, more and more links — and longer ones — and many more instances of abbreviations.

In the PITMANSCRIPT on the following pages there is considerable vowel omission. Nevertheless, individual writers will probably show even fewer vowels than are included in passages **1** to **70**. This is because these pages have been written with the needs of a large number of scriptors in mind, whereas the individual need think only of himself: he is under no necessity to show any vowels that he feels he can dispense with.

In actual practice the most frequently written words will vary from person to person, because occupations and interests vary. The words most frequently used by the members of the staff of a factory which concentrates on the manufacture of footwear differ from those used in a firm of management consultants. Each scriptor will, therefore, find himself writing certain words automatically in an abbreviated form. Absolute uniformity of notes should not be looked for or expected, because individuality is built into PITMANSCRIPT: it is designed to serve individual needs.

Nor will absolute uniformity be found in the PITMANSCRIPT which follows. Context often influences the inclusion or exclusion of a vowel. Repetition also affects it. If a curious word like *gazumping* was suddenly used, a natural reaction would be to vocalize it. To include the vowels a second or third time would be unnecessary and time wasting, and *gzmp* could be safely used. Therefore scriptors can, if they wish, take vowel omission several stages further than has been done in this book.

Abbreviation — that is, writing only the first part of a word — will also vary from individual to individual — and for the same reasons as those given above. What is written most often will tend to be written in the shortest possible way: *a* for *advertisement*, *acm* for *accommodation*, *df* for *different*, *dfc* for *difficulty*, *ime* for *immediately* are a few examples.

Such abbreviated forms have not, however, been made part of the basic system — because they are not *essential* learning. The writer is free to abbreviate a lot or a little as he prefers, and notes should not be considered wrong if abbreviation strikes an observer as being either excessive or too restrained. The important point is: can the writer read what he has written, and were the notes taken at the desired speed? If the answer is "yes", then the work is satisfactory. As I mentioned in the case of vowels, there need not be absolute consistency. Scriptors will be influenced by the speed of dictation and by context, and can vary their writing accordingly. In the script which follows in these pages, it will be noticed that a word is sometimes written rather fully at the outset but is abbreviated when repeated. This seems commonsense, and writers should try to develop this habit.

Another way in which writers can speed up their writing is to have their own PITMANSCRIPT special signs. No list of special signs exists beyond the 24 taught in the *Basic Text* because it is believed better to leave the writer unburdened with *having* to learn a great many special signs; he is, in fact, quite free to short-cut at will.

Some writers may, for instance, adopt *q* for *quite*; some may like the use of *g* for *good*; *by* might well be adopted for *beyond* (the word *by* is, of course *bi*); *object* can become *obj* in fast writing, and *respect* will most probably be abbreviated to *rspc*.

Options of this kind are open to the writer. The important thing is for him to remember his own special signs and make a habit of using them.

The use of abbreviation will vary with context. If in the course of a passage the words *hire purchase* occurred once only, the writer would probably write the words fully. If, however, the passage dealt solely with hire purchase, it would be sensible to abbreviate and write ...*H.P.*... (capitals to indicate that the full words were required, ...*hp*... being used when the reader dictates h.p.), or ...... or some other abbreviation.

The reader of this book should not, therefore, search for utter consistency in the PITMANSCRIPT in these pages – or elsewhere – as the writing may vary with the circumstances of the passage. It might even, perhaps, vary with the mood of the moment, or the feeling of haste or leisure. There is sometimes an artistic enjoyment to be found in writing fully and meticulously, while at other times the aspect of speed will be more enticing.

Most scriptors use the initial tick for *we* when a second *w* follows, as ...... *we will,* ...... *we would;* and also the disjoined downstroke for *m* when another *m* immediately follows, as ...... *memory.* These short cuts were suggested in the Preface to *Skill Book 2*, and some writers have carried the idea further, writing ...... *paper,* ...... *vivid,* ...... *baboon,* etc. There are even scriptors who use the tick for *we* in all cases: ...... *we hope,* ...... *we like,* etc.

A repeated letter can usually be omitted medially as in ...... *probable* and ...... *remember. Apoplexy* is, fortunately, not a common word, but if it were it could be written .... We have here the same rule: write what you need for accurate reading back.

If a writer decides to use a disjoined sign for a prefix or suffix, great care should be taken to ensure that it cannot be read as a separate word. Some scriptors favour the use of ...*c*... for *inter/intro,* ...*u*... for *under*, and ...*x*... for *extra.* If such short cuts are adopted, I advise the writer to place the single letter *above* the line so that it does not look like *I, you* or *ex-*: ...... *introduction,* ...... *interest,* ...... *undertake,* ...... *understand,* ...... *extramural,* ...... *extraordinary.* Others use a final ...*m*... for *ment* (joined or disjoined). This is quite satisfactory so long as the writer is familiar with the type of material he is writing, and does not use such devices in a haphazard manner.

There is seldom any need to show final *t* following *c*; ...*ac*... *act,* ...*fac*... *fact,* ...... *correct*, are quite adequate representations. On the other hand, there is little or no advantage in omitting the final stroke for *n, l* or *r*. Not only are these strokes designed to carry the hand forward, but their omission might cause difficulty when transcribing. PITMANSCRIPT in its basic form is extremely legible, and any personal variation that it is proposed to adopt must first be well tested for its effect on legibility.

And now we come to the use of links. It cannot be too strongly stressed that their use is optional. On the other hand, neither can it be too strongly emphasized that their use is a great aid to facile and fast writing. In the Appendix (pp. 131–136) you will find a list of some of the links which have occurred in the course of the PITMANSCRIPT in this book. The links given are examples only andscannot be considered exhaustive. Indeed, it would be impossible to exhaust the possibilities because there is no limit to possible linking. The best rule is: link when you can, and join special signs at every opportunity as this is an aid to rapid transcription. The signs for *a, of, to, the, is, as, not,* ought to be joined whenever possible, and "lowered" to show clearly that a link has been written. For instance, compare: 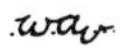 *way of* with 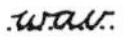 *wave.* Remember also that the special signs make distinctive links. For instance, compare:  *you are not* with  *urn*;  *is not* with 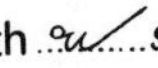 *sun.*

The reader of the script given in passages **1** to **70** must regard it as a suggested example only. A few comments are made after most of the passages to draw attention to points of interest; and, as each passage stands by itself, it happens occasionally that the same point is mentioned more than once because teachers may dictate the pieces in any order they please. Writers must not forget one point – their writing must be neat and light. Digging into the paper is tiring and time wasting. A light quick style must be cultivated if the advantages of writing PITMANSCRIPT are to be developed to the full.

PERSONAL SCRIPTING

There has been no extended use of personalized short cuts in passages **1** to **70**, which are intended to be of general interest and useful to all classes of writers, even those using PITMANSCRIPT for jotting down notes, shopping lists, etc.

Passages **71** to **100** have been differently treated, however. Six scriptors have each written five of these passages, and have been free to write in the style that each personally prefers. You will observe that there is a varying use of links and abbreviations but *no* abuse of the basic principles of the system. The writers are:

71 to **75**: the author
76 to **80**: Mr. Bert Canning

81 to **85**: Mr. Albert Elsegood
86 to **90**: Mr. Victor Hurrion
91 to **95**: Mr. Stanley Bartholomew
96 to **100**: Miss Diane Hynds.

E.D.S.

PUBLISHERS' NOTE

The publishers acknowledge with sincere thanks the permission of the following Examining Bodies to use a selection of their Shorthand Speed Tests:

East Midland Educational Union
London Chamber of Commerce
Pitman Examinations Institute
Royal Society of Arts
Union of Lancashire and Cheshire Institutes
Welsh Joint Education Committee
Yorkshire Council for Further Education.

1

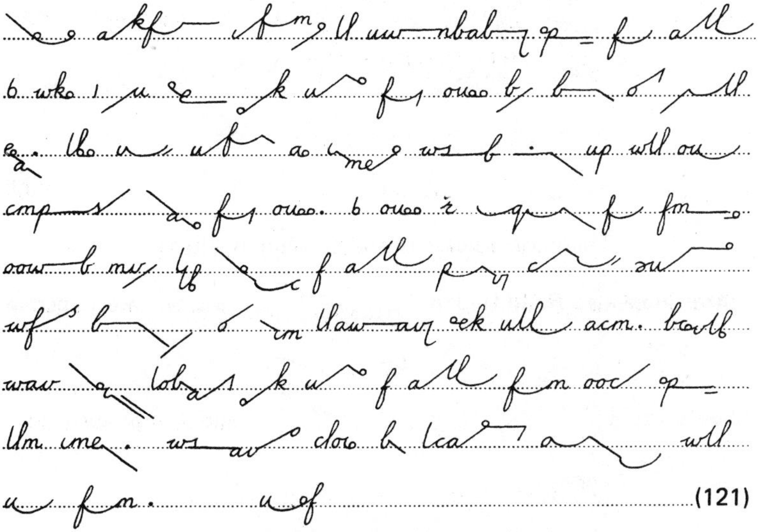

(121)

Union of Lancashire and Cheshire Institutes

Links to note are .... and .... Vowel omission is seen in ...., ..., ..., ..., ..., and some short-cuts are ...., ..., ...

2

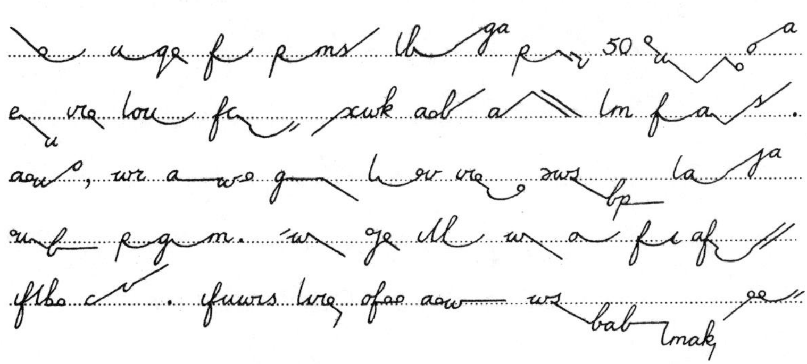

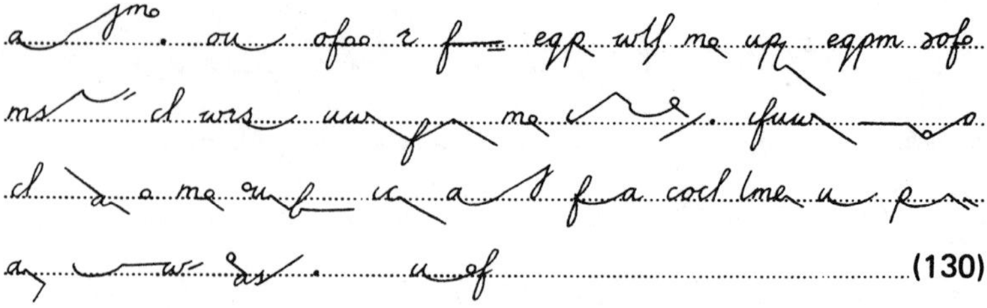

(130)

Union of Lancashire and Cheshire Institutes

Links: Repeated *R* omitted in  are joined in  etc.

Short-cuts:  and  for *-ment* in 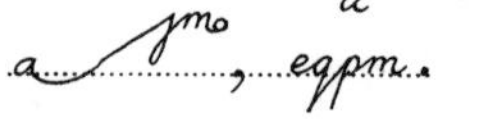

3

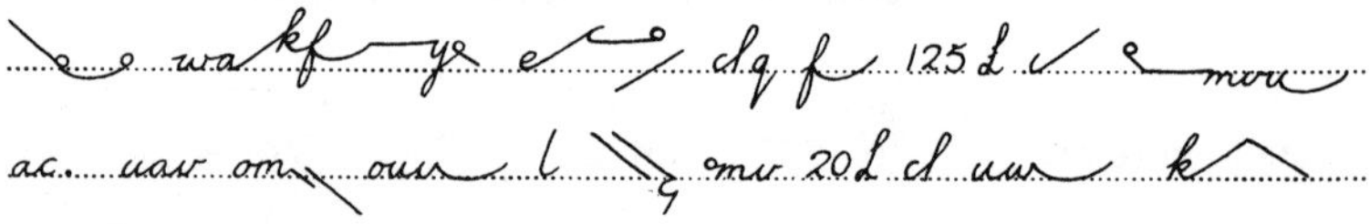

(150)

Union of Lancashire and Cheshire Institutes

Links:

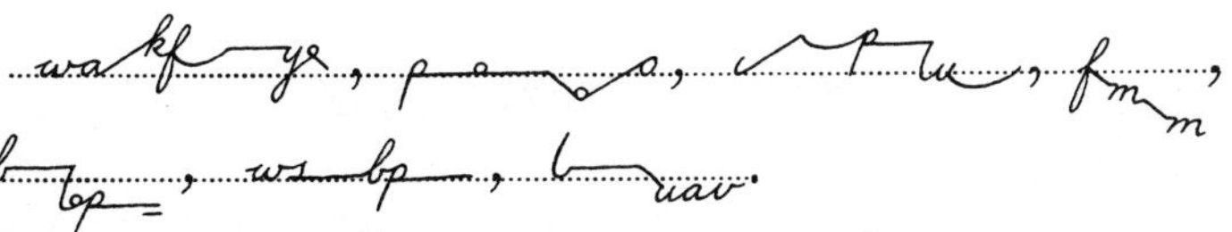

Short-cuts:

4

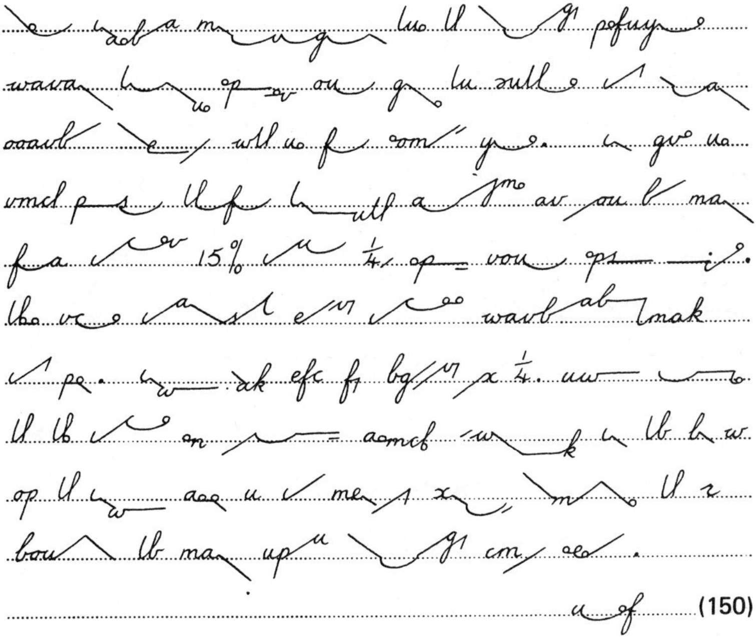

(150)

Pitman Examinations Institute

Links:

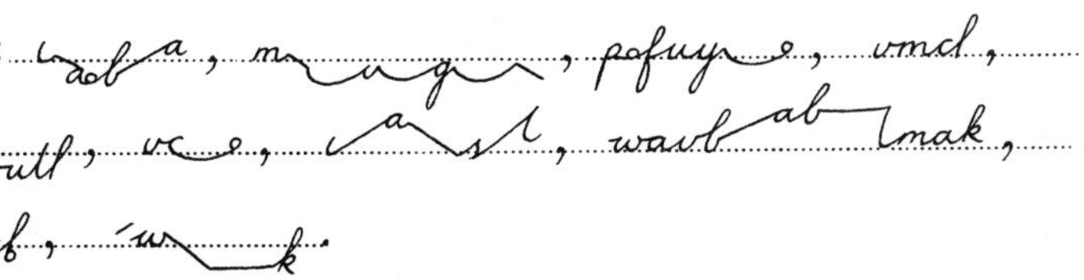

Short-cuts:

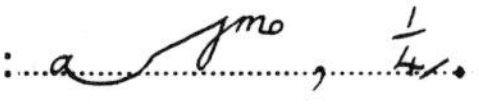

5

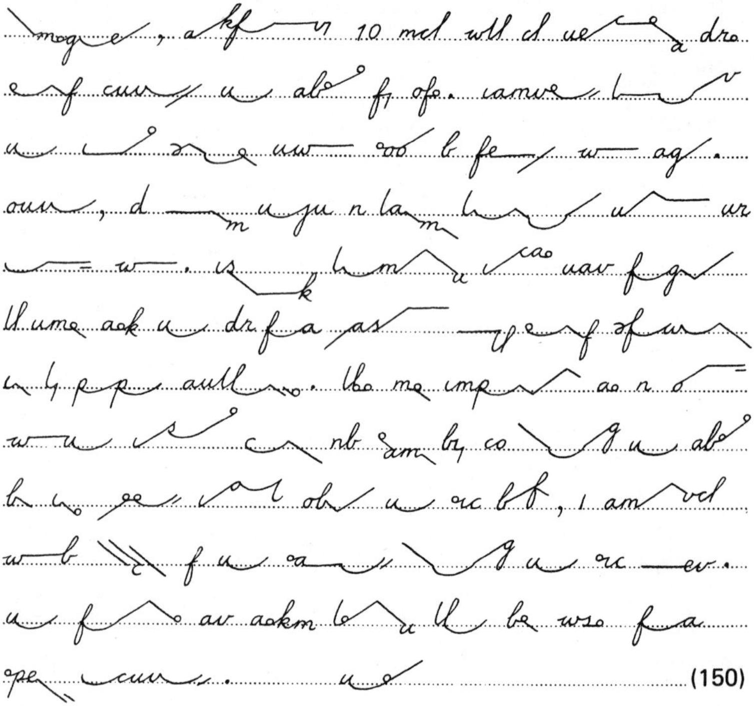

(150)

Royal Society of Arts

Links: 

6

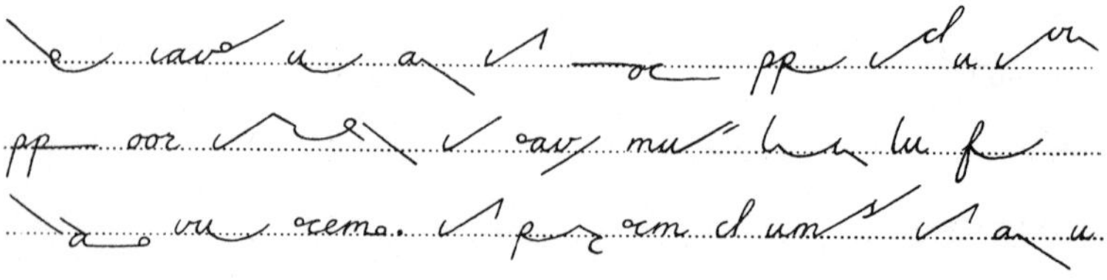

(150)

Pitman Examinations Institute

Vowel omission is seen in , , , , , , ; also , , , when repeated.

Links: , , , , .

is used for 400. Note also for *thousand* and for *million*.

7

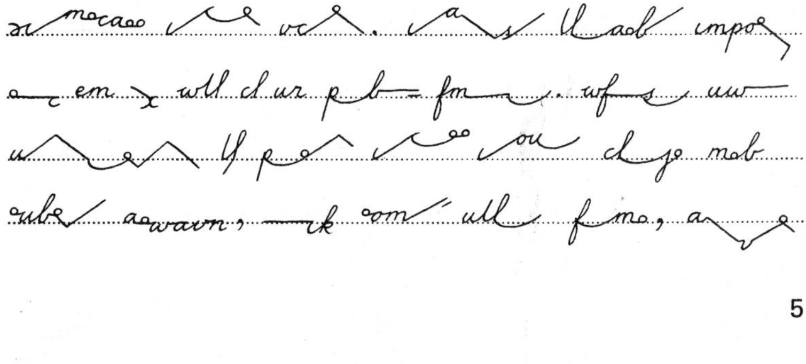

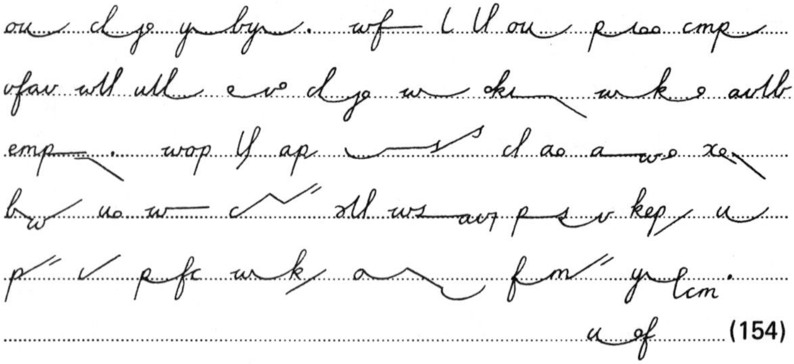

(154)

Yorkshire Council for Further Education

Links: 

Omission of dot H: 

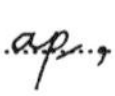 etc. Note also 

8

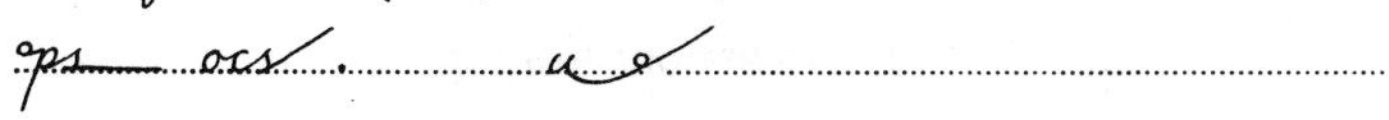 (160)

Royal Society of Arts

Links: 

Candidates and *application* are cut to 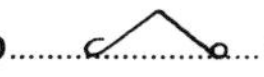 and  when repeated, and other abbreviations are: 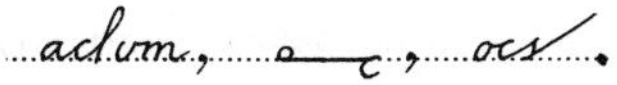

9

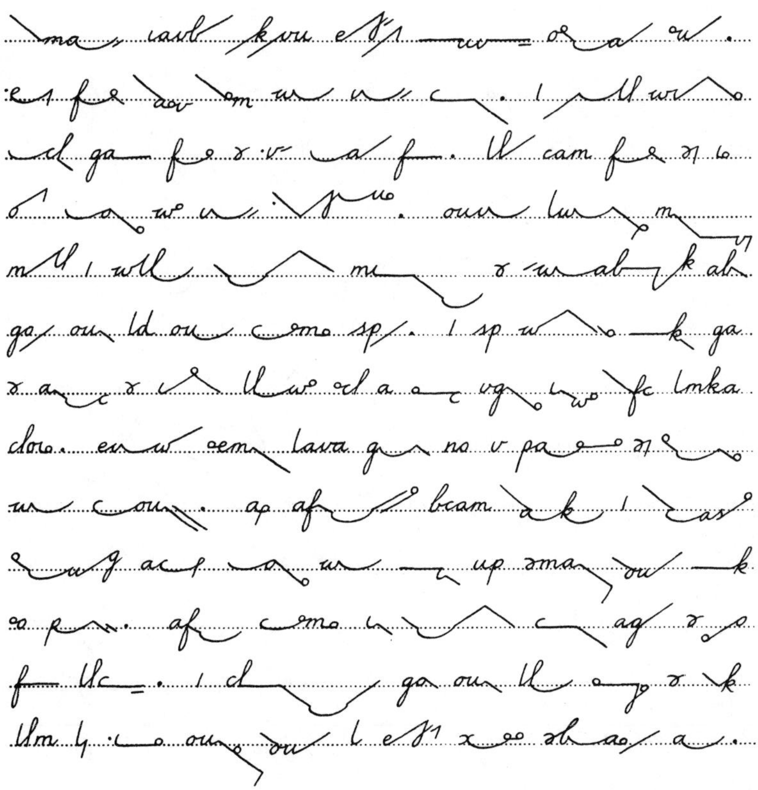

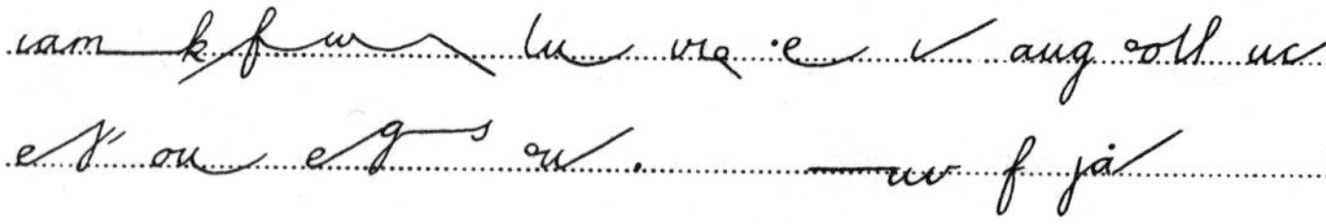 (180)

Pitman Examinations Institute

Note that other forms can be joined to  (ing): , . Note also the use of the dash for *we* in .

Vowels are unnecessary in, for instance,  where the meaning is obvious.

10

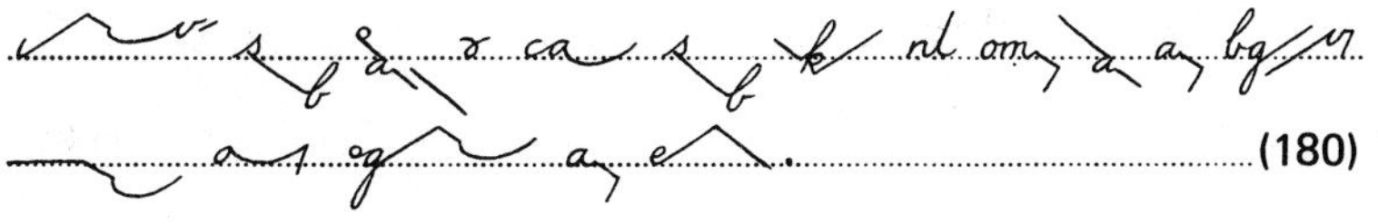 (180)

Yorkshire Council for Further Education

Short-cuts: 

There are several examples of vowel omission: 

 etc.

Links: 

Note also 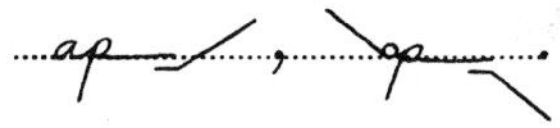

11

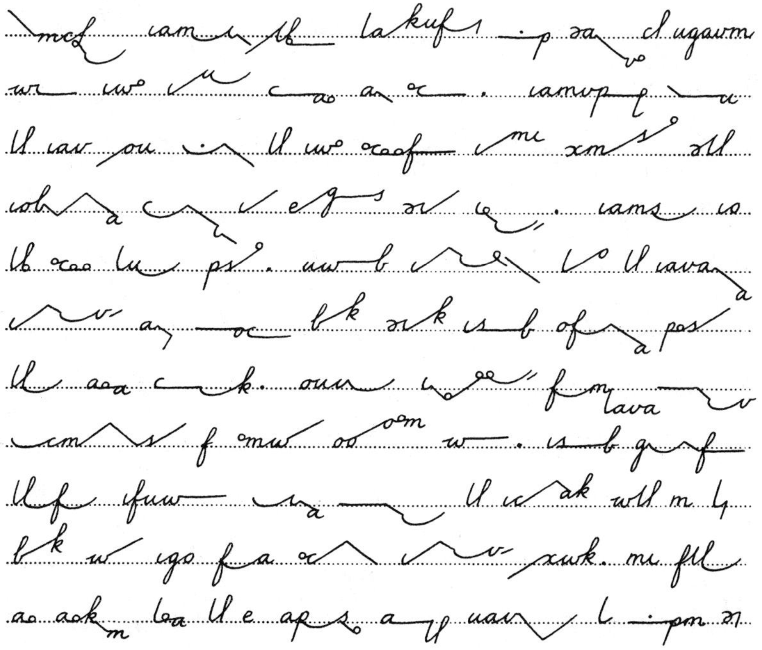

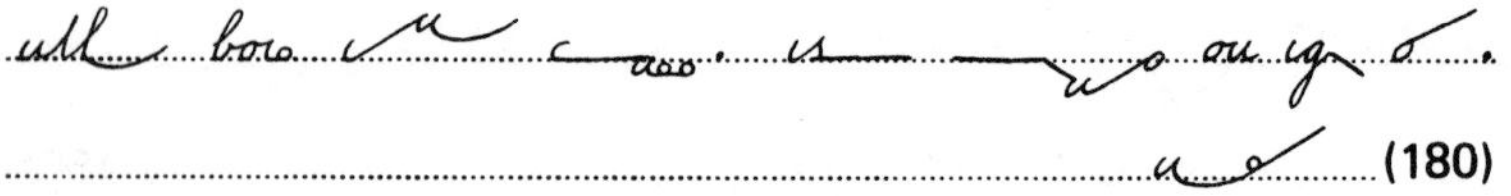

(180)

Pitman Examinations Institute

Examples of vowel omission are: , , , , ; and H is omitted in and .

Some links: , , , , .

12

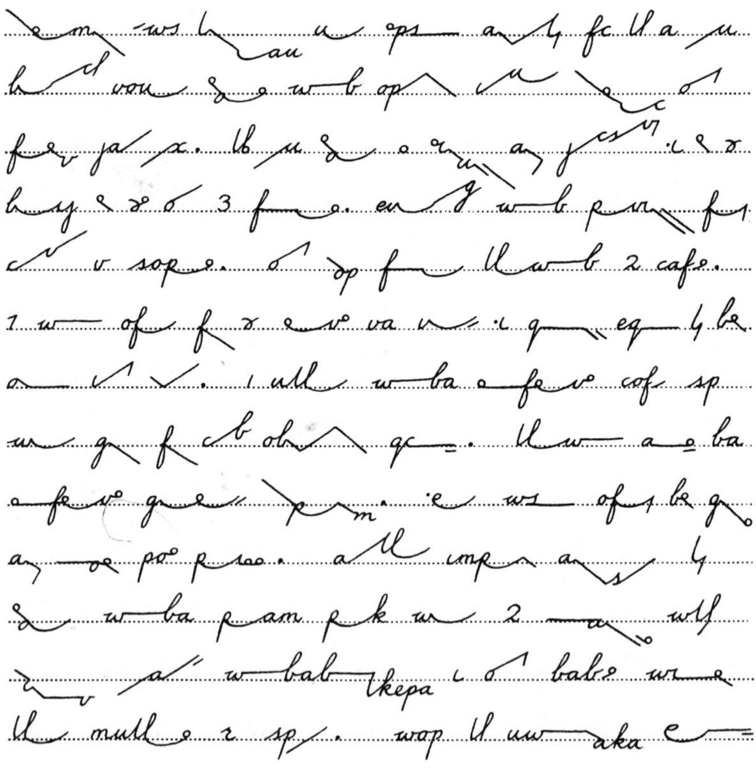

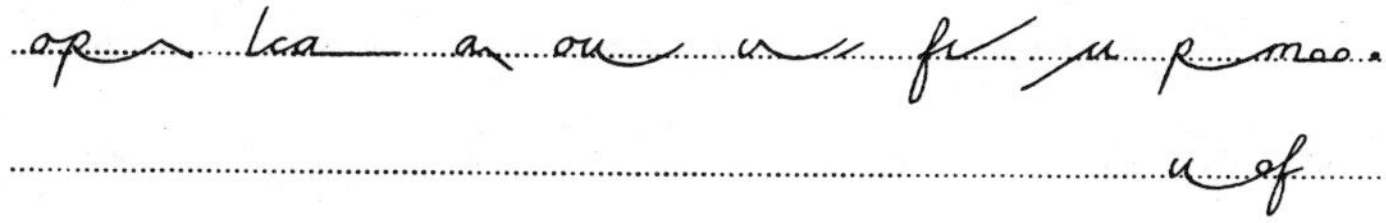

(180)

Pitman Examinations Institute

Links: 

Vowel Omissions: 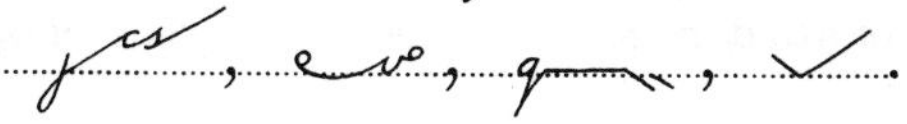

Note also  for .

13

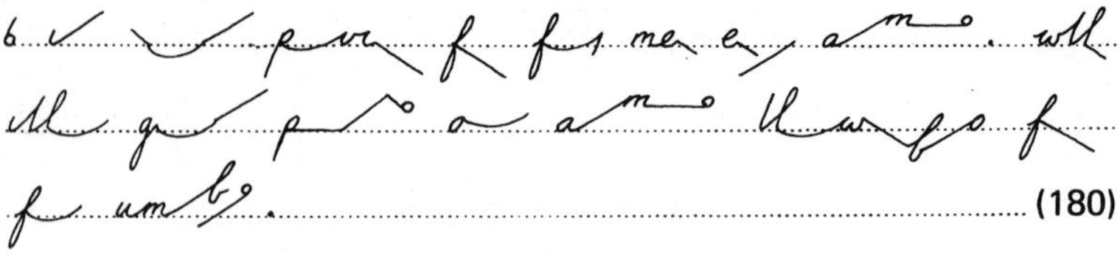

(180)

Royal Society of Arts

Vowels are omitted in  and 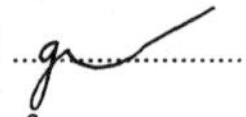 upon repetition.

Links: 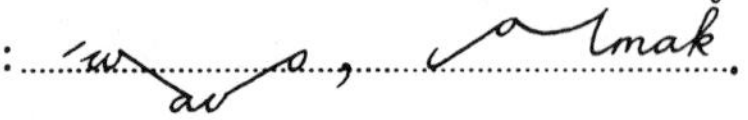

14

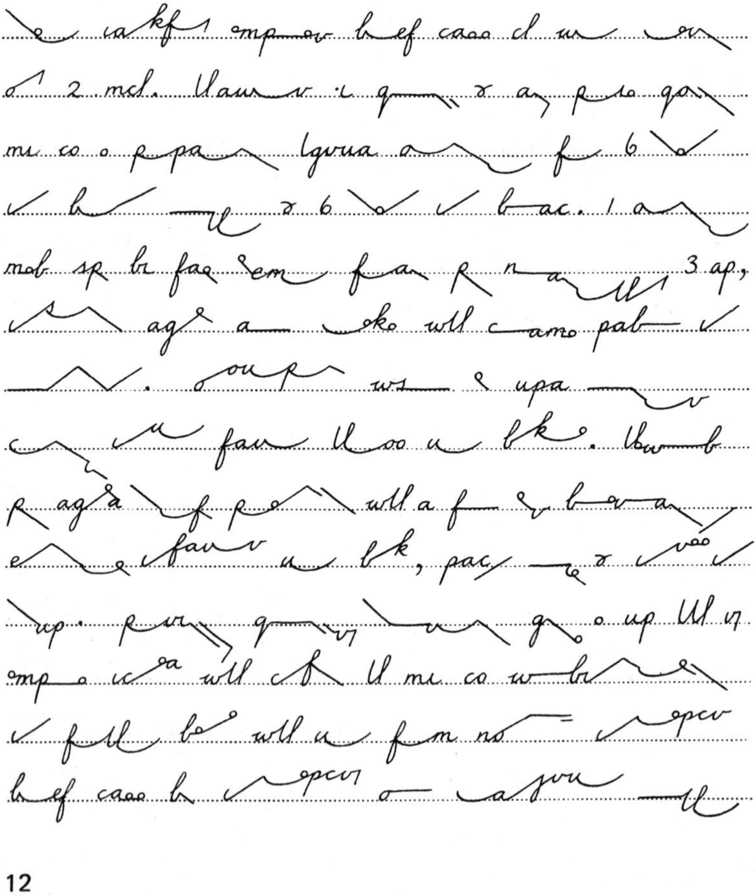

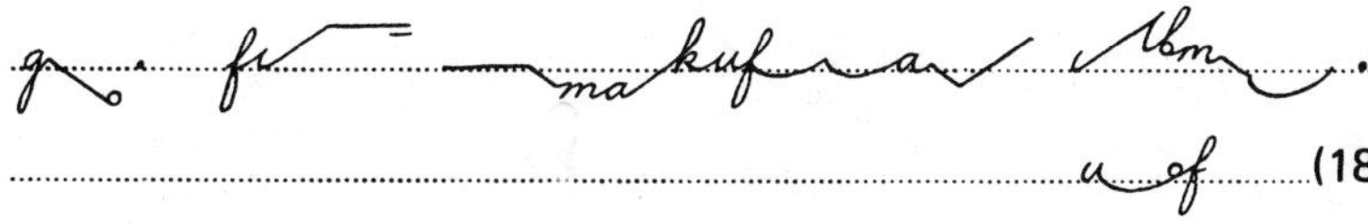

(180)

Royal Society of Arts

Links:

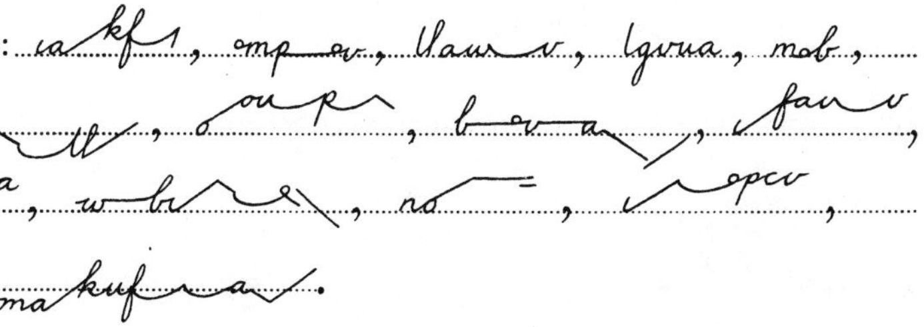

15

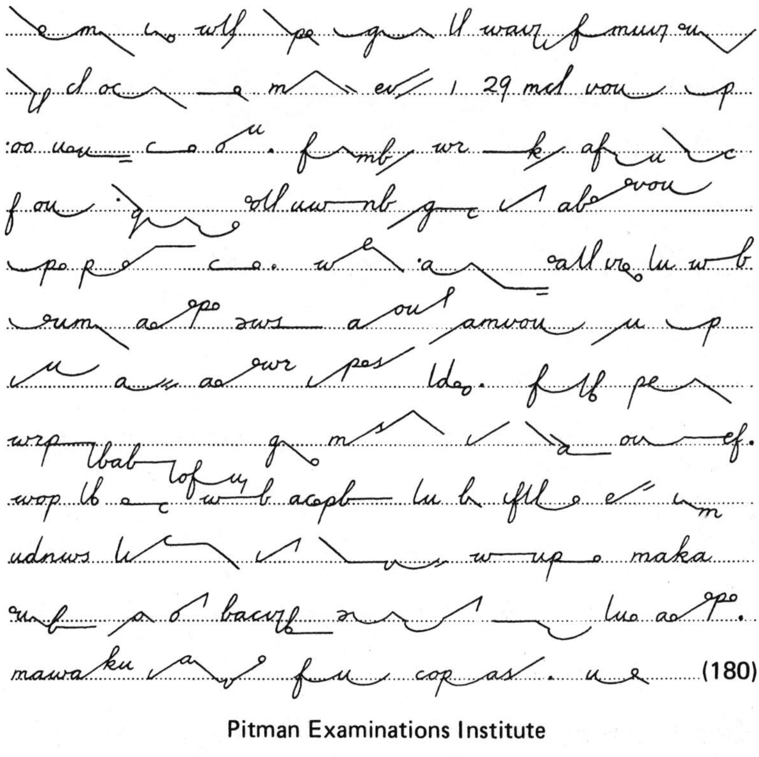

(180)

Pitman Examinations Institute

Some longer links are 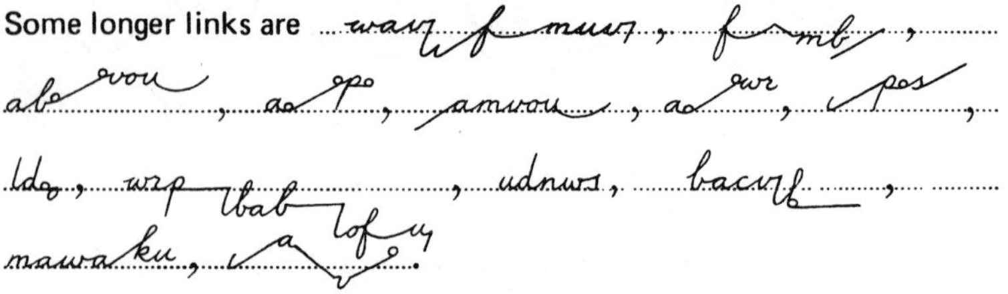

 and  are examples of short-cuts.

16

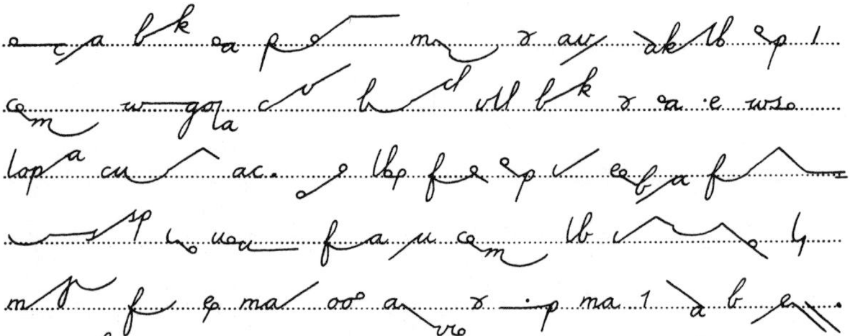 (180)

Yorkshire Council for Further Education

Some abbreviations are ,  and . 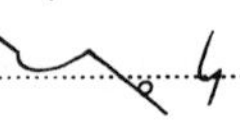 is cut to … when repeated. Vowels are not needed in …, …, … . Note … .

17

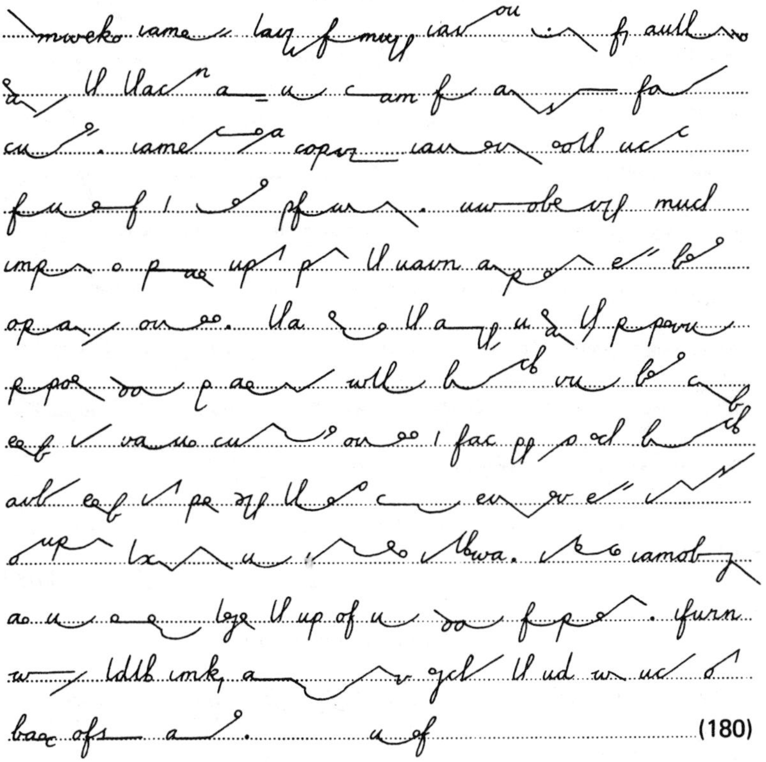

(180)

Pitman Examinations Institute

Links:

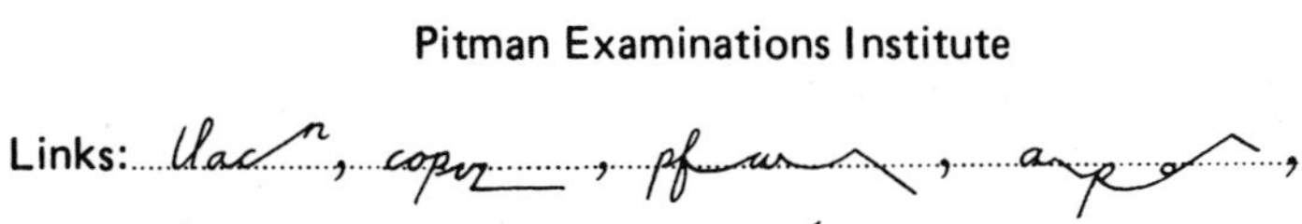

… is a sufficient representation for *establish-ed-ment*, as misreading is improbable.

18

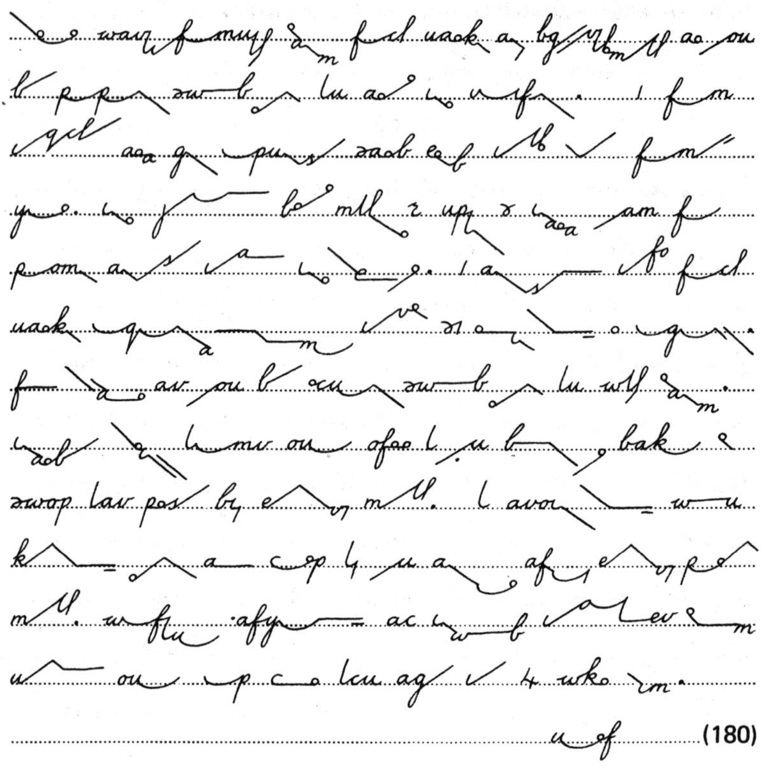

(180)

Pitman Examinations Institute

Links: 

Notice  for *information*.

19

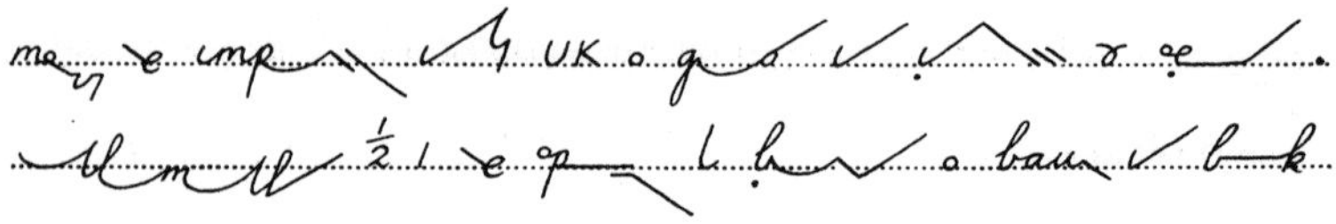

(180)

Royal Society of Arts

U.K. can be used for *United Kingdom* and uk for *U.K.*

Note  and .

20

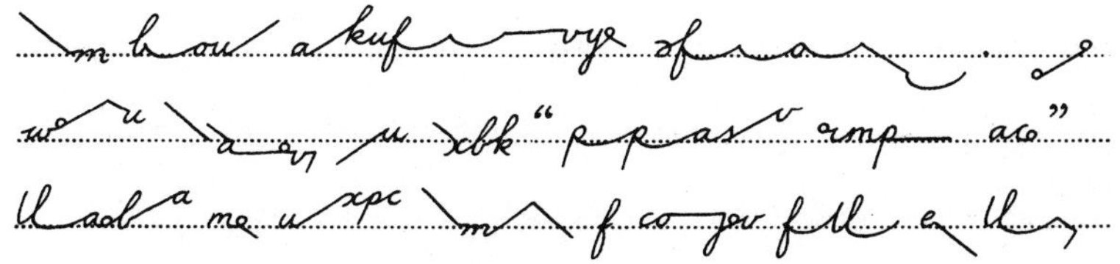

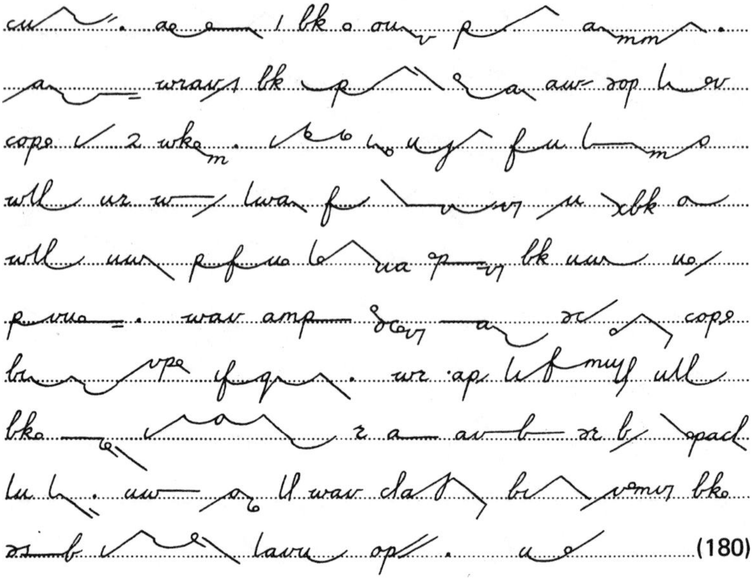

(180)

Pitman Examinations Institute

Links used above include

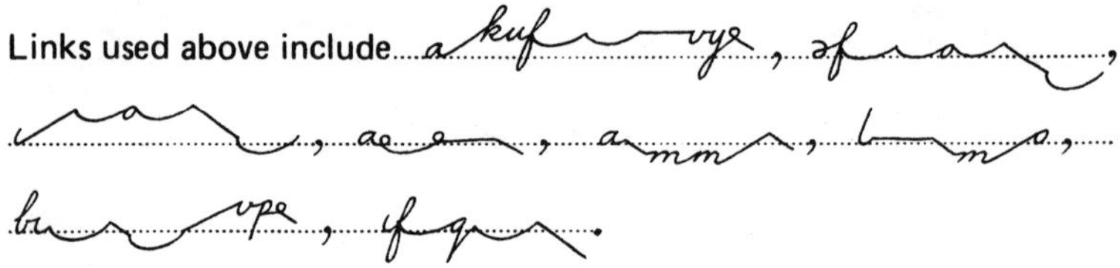

21

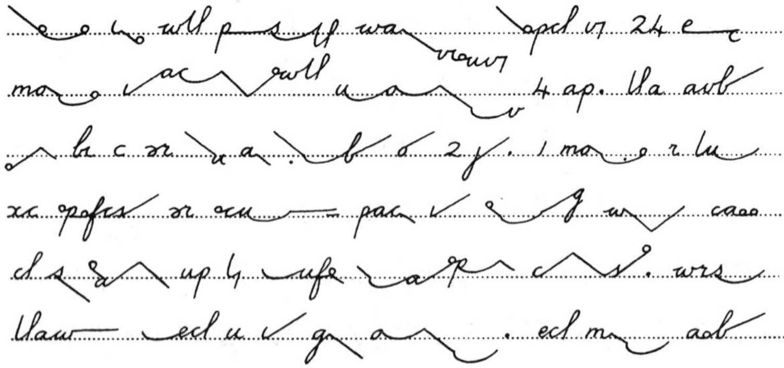

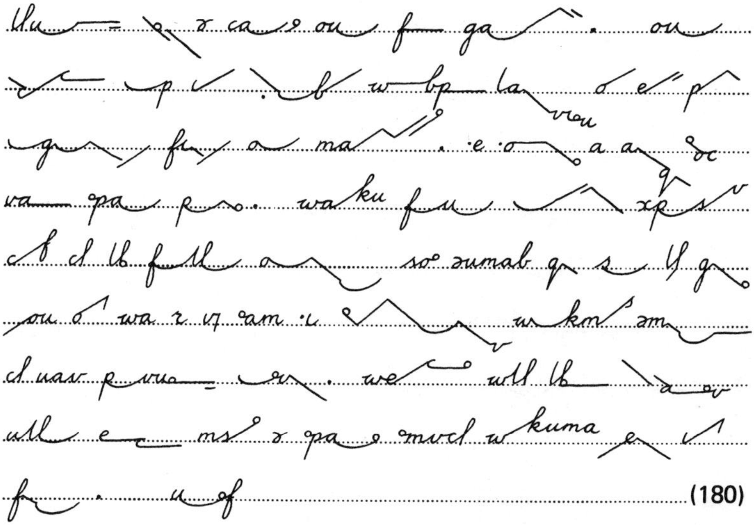

(180)

Royal Society of Arts

Some abbreviated forms are , , , , , . The vowel is omitted from when repeated.

Links: , , , .

22

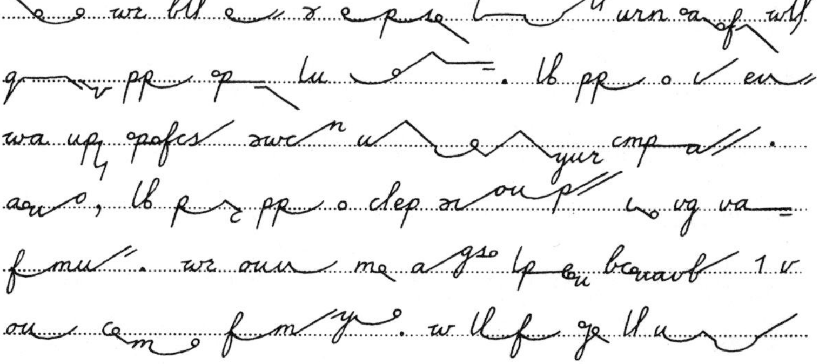

(180)

Pitman Examinations Institute

Vowels are unnecessary in  and .

Some links are 

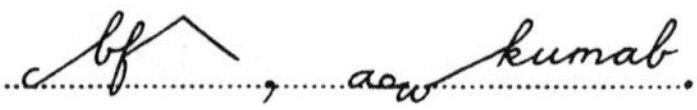

23

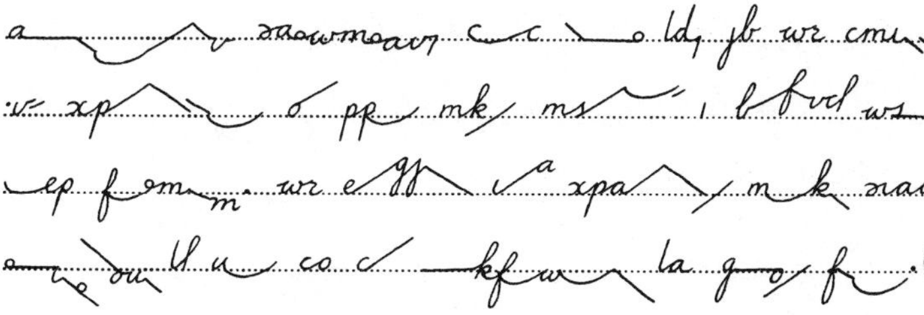

(180)

Royal Society of Arts

Context allows vowels to be omitted in

Abbreviations are

Links:

24

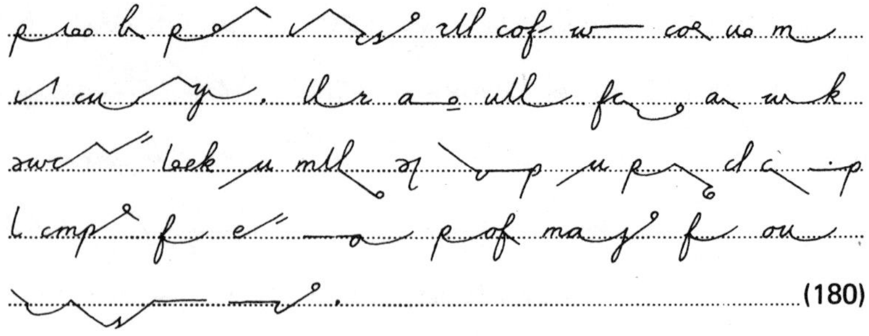

(180)

Royal Society of Arts

Note 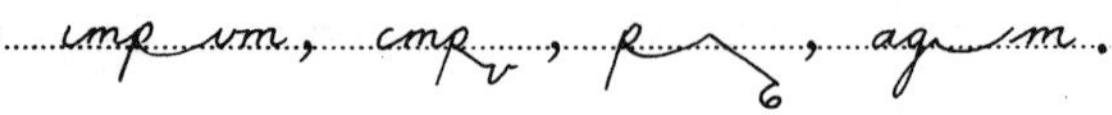

25

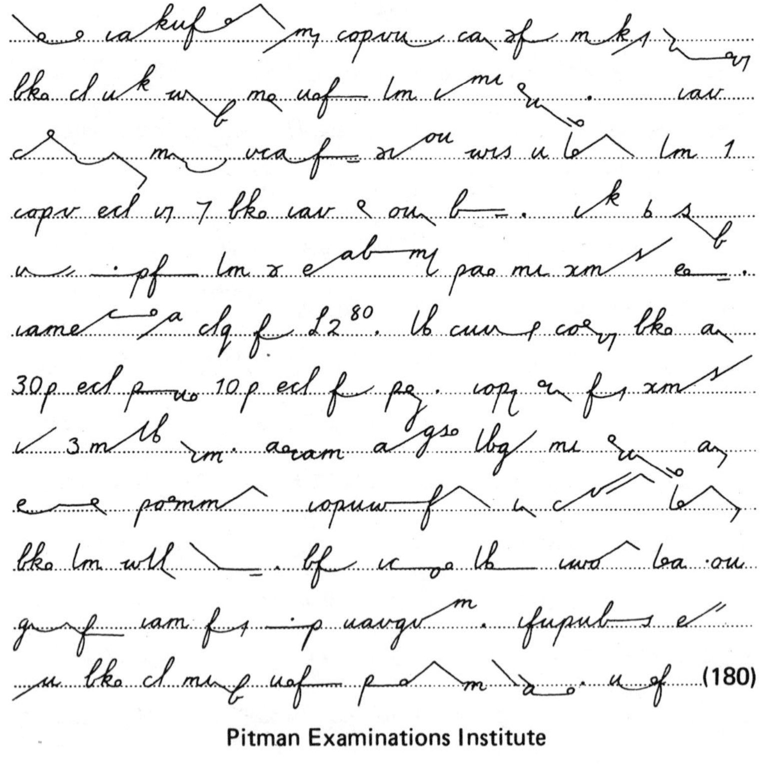

(180)

Pitman Examinations Institute

is adequate for *catalogue* in this context. In the vowel is medial and need not be shown, but note . Some links are

26

(180)

Pitman Examinations Institute

Some vowel omissions are , , , . The vowel should be inserted in and

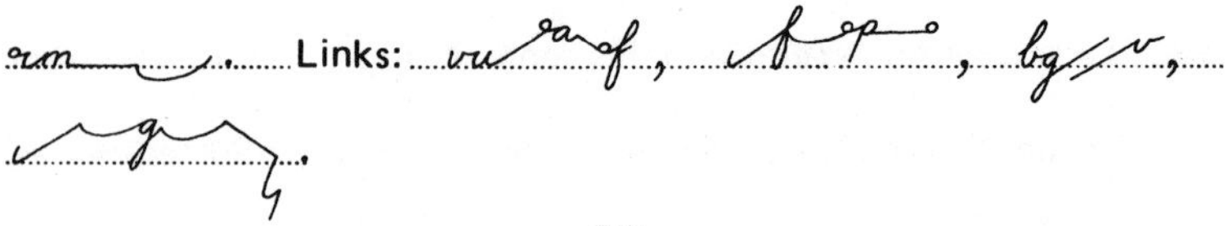

27

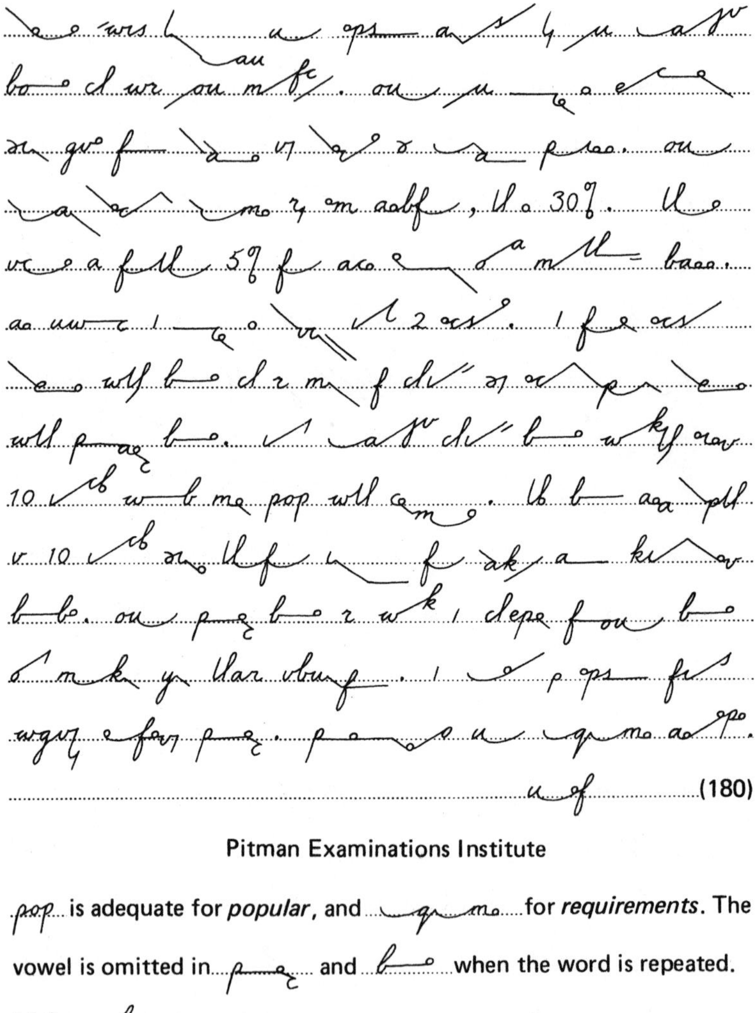

(180)

Pitman Examinations Institute

... is adequate for *popular*, and ... for *requirements*. The vowel is omitted in ... and ... when the word is repeated.

Links: ...

28

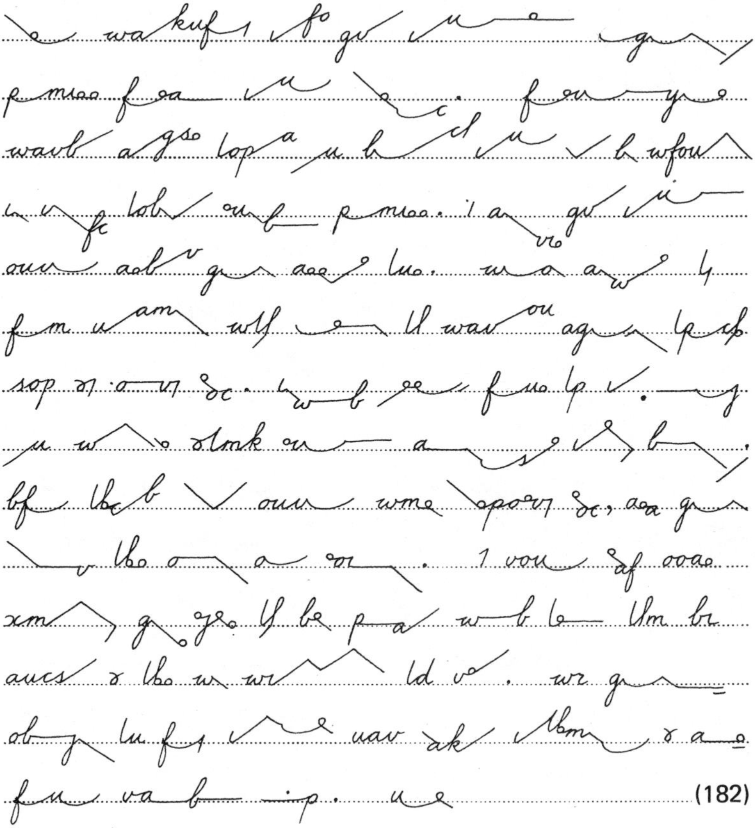

(182)

Union of Lancashire and Cheshire Institutes

Some links used here are 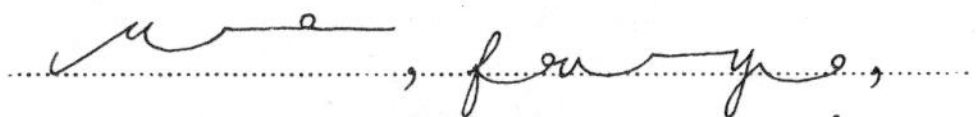, 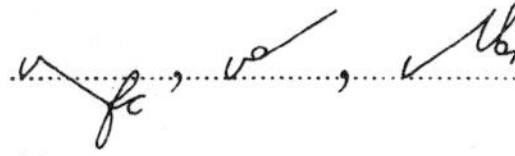, 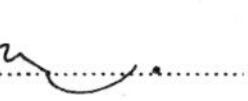. *Information* is cut to 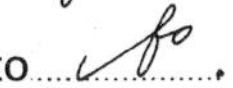.

No vowel is needed in  and  as the meaning is obvious.

29

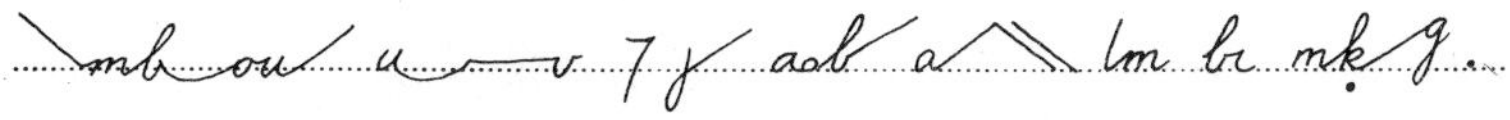

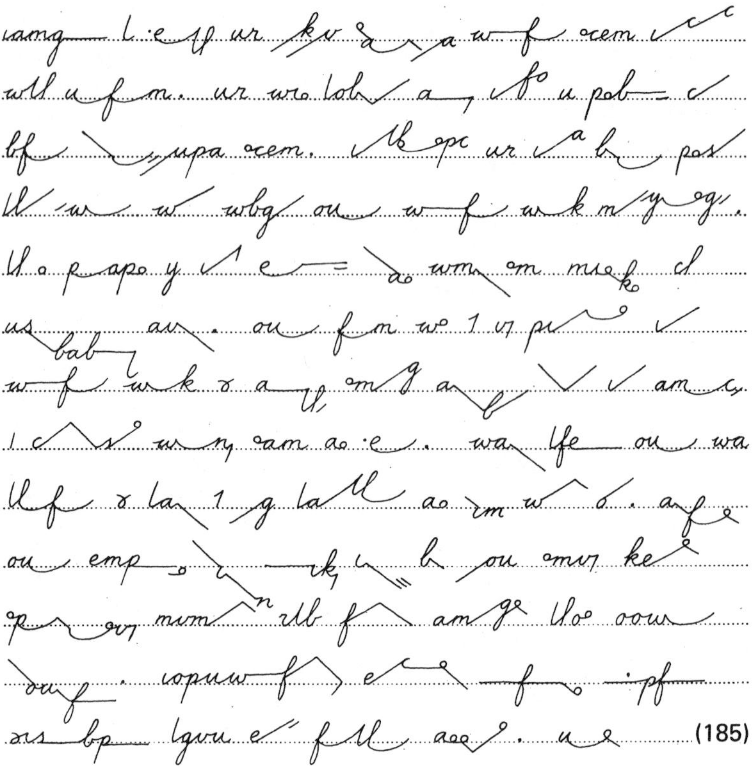

(185)

Union of Lancashire and Cheshire Institutes

Find and *found* can usually be written 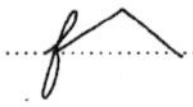 as context is normally a sufficient guide. Note the links 

30

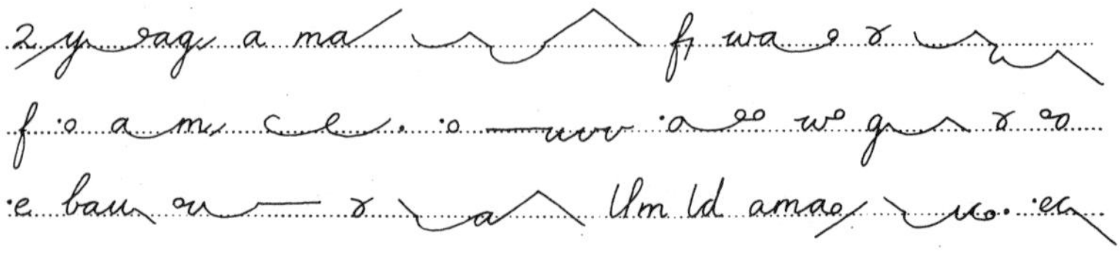

(188)

Union of Lancashire and Cheshire Institutes

Literary passages generally require more vowels than commercial material. Always vocalize 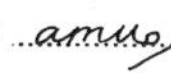 and .

31

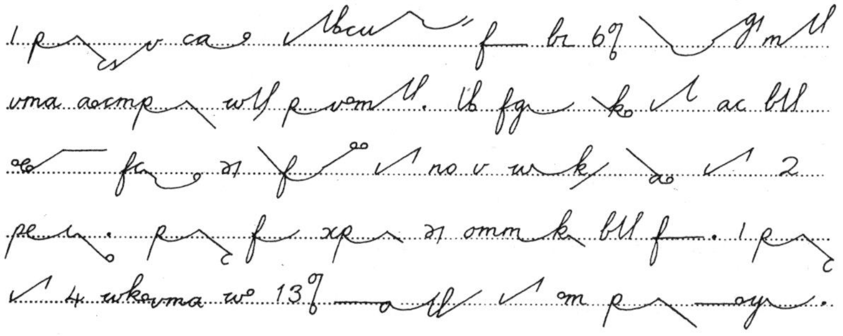

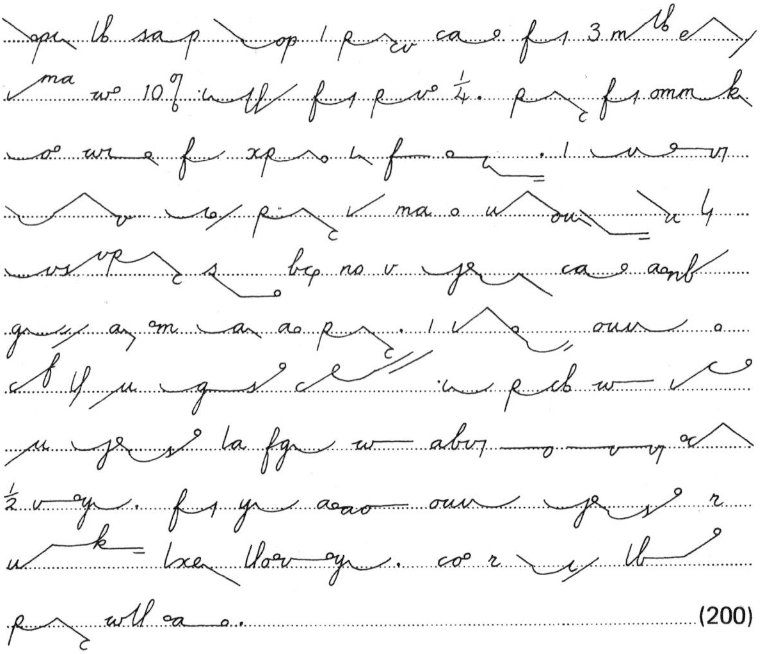

(200)

Royal Society of Arts

Links: 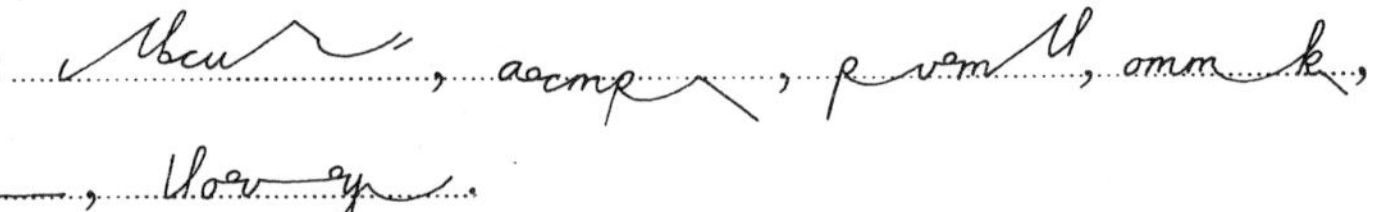

32

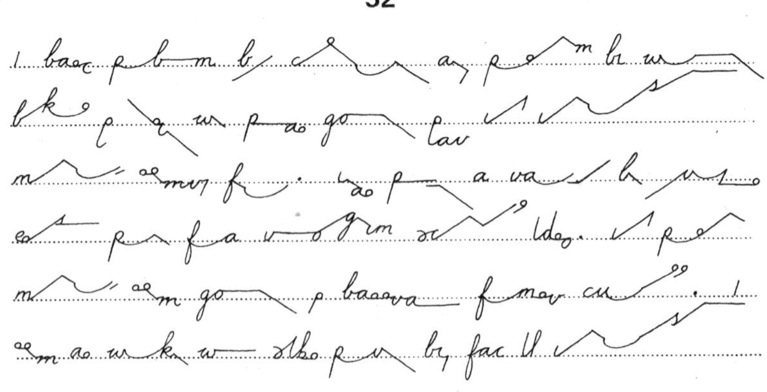

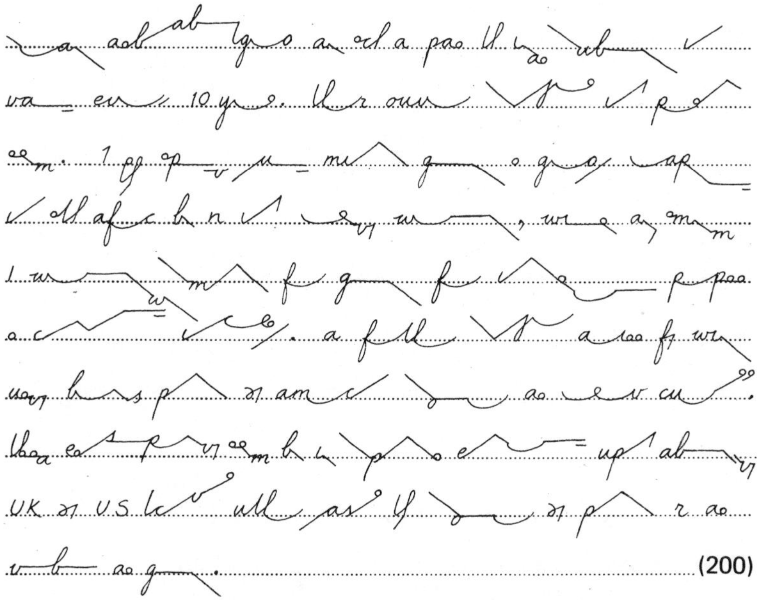

(200)

Yorkshire Council for Further Education

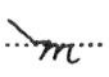 is used for *time* in 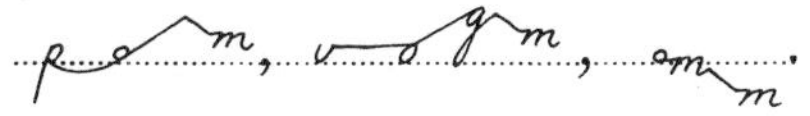

33

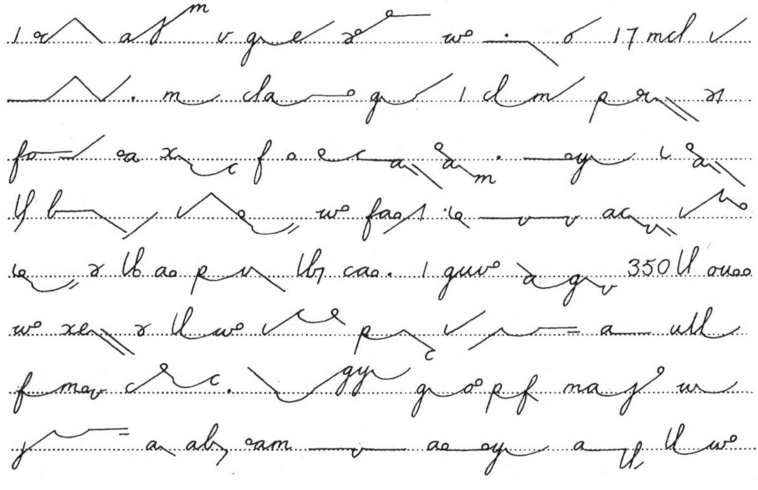

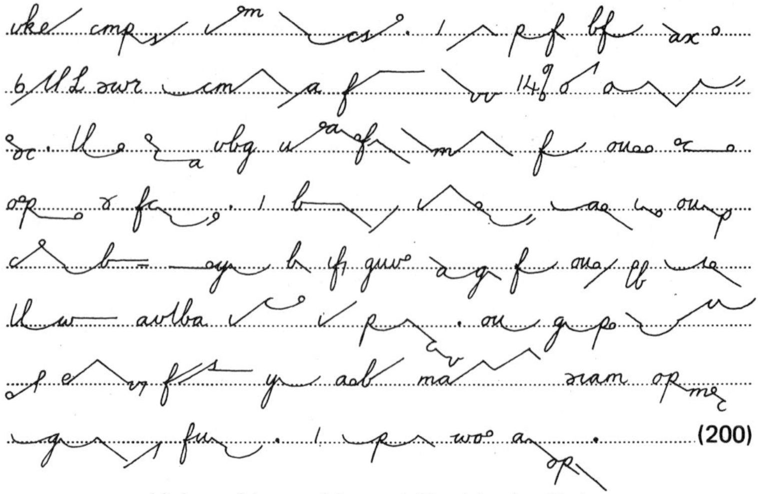

(200)

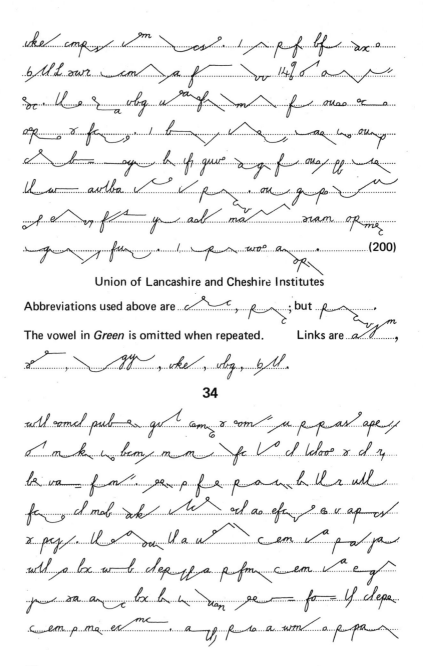

Union of Lancashire and Cheshire Institutes

Abbreviations used above are 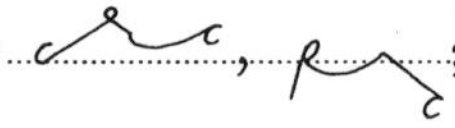; but 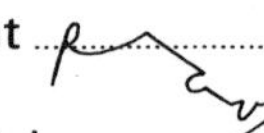.

The vowel in *Green* is omitted when repeated. Links are 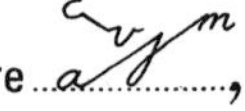,

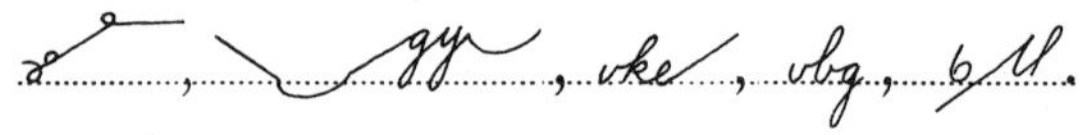

34

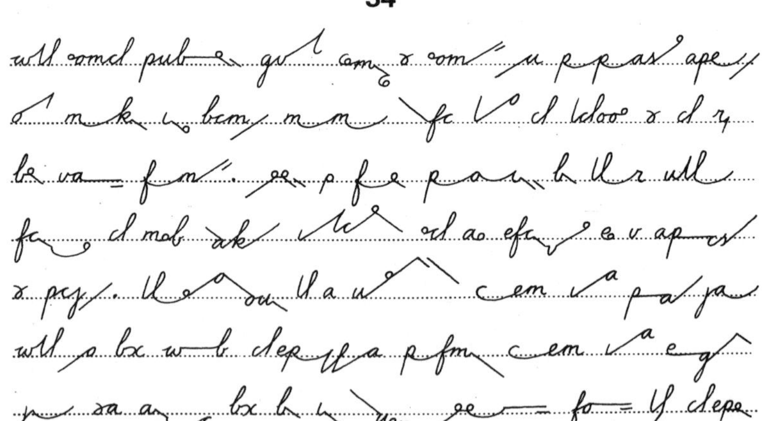

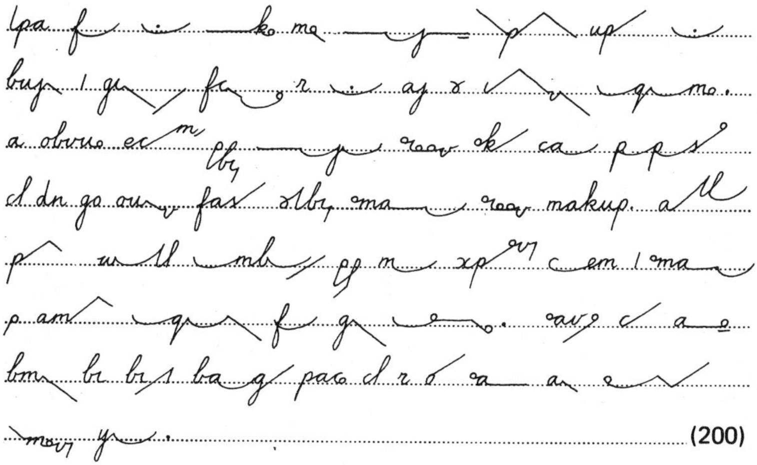

(200)

Yorkshire Council for Further Education

Vowels are omitted when the word is obvious or is repeated: 

35

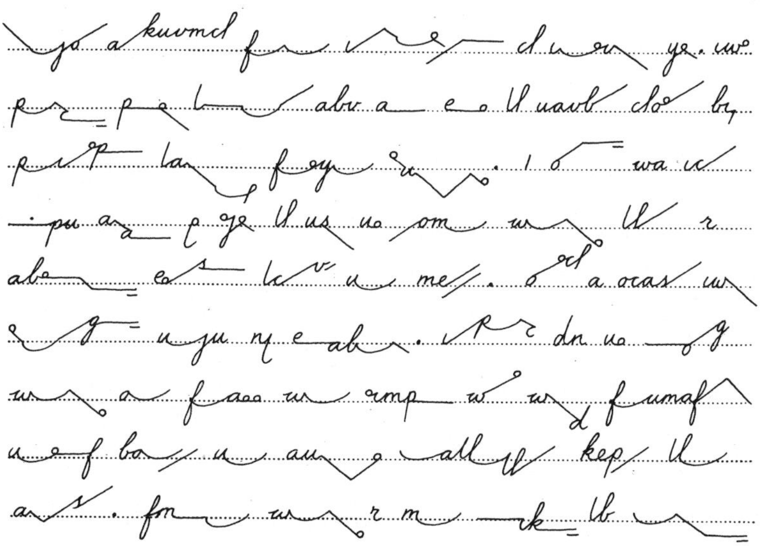

(210)

Pitman Examinations Institute

Use either ½ or :af for *half*. In links ____ is sufficient for *letter*.

36

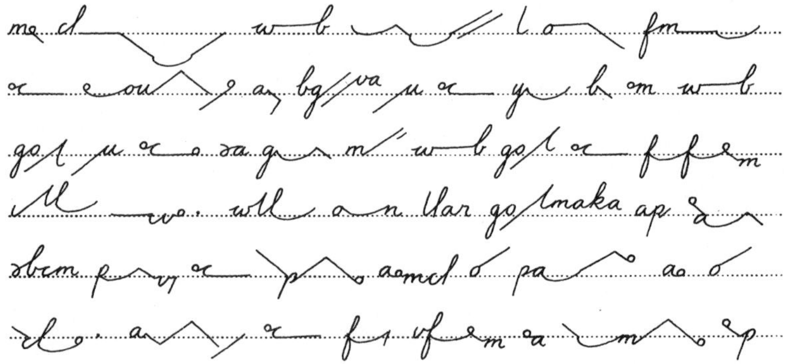

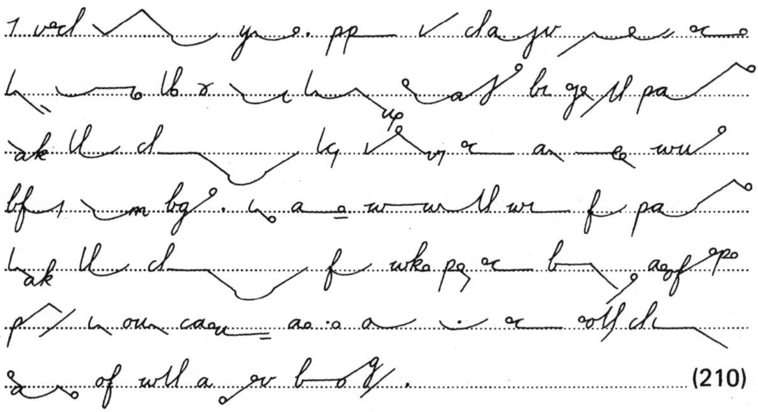

(210)

Yorkshire Council for Further Education

Links: 

37

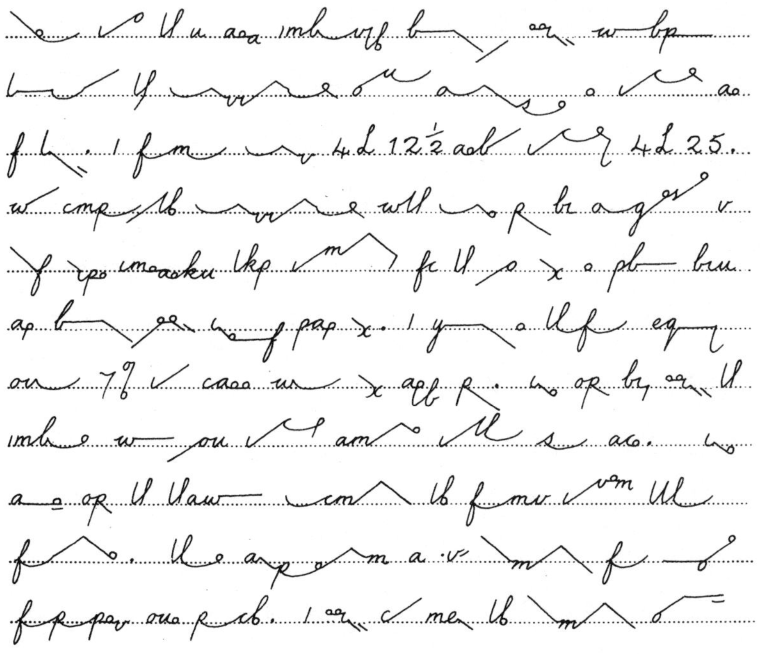

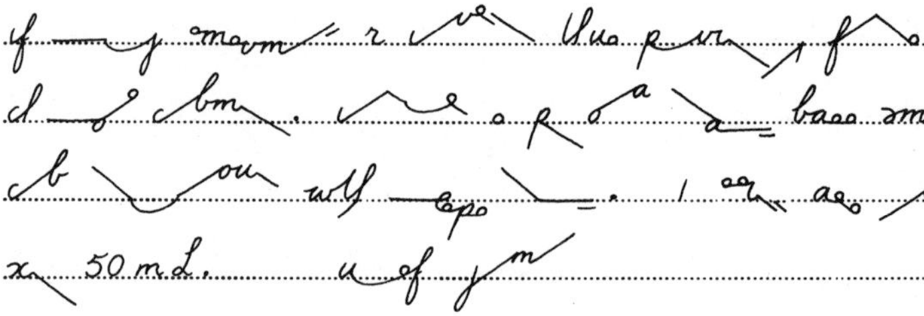

(210)

Pitman Examinations Institute

Links to note: (when repeated). Short-cuts:

38

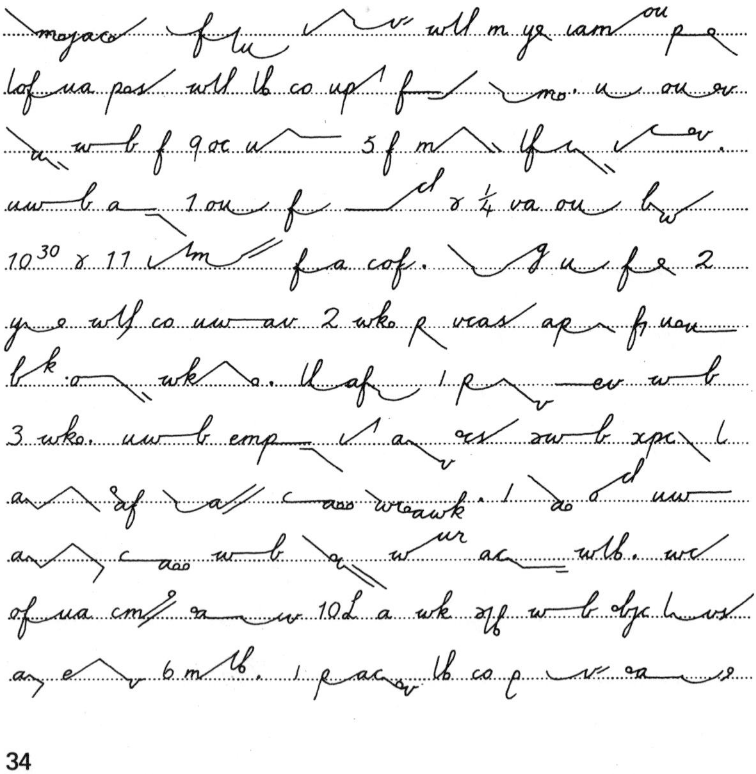

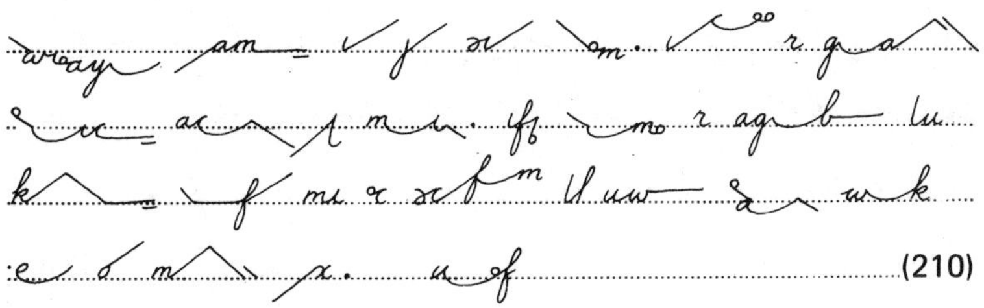

(210)

Pitman Examinations Institute

Note the links 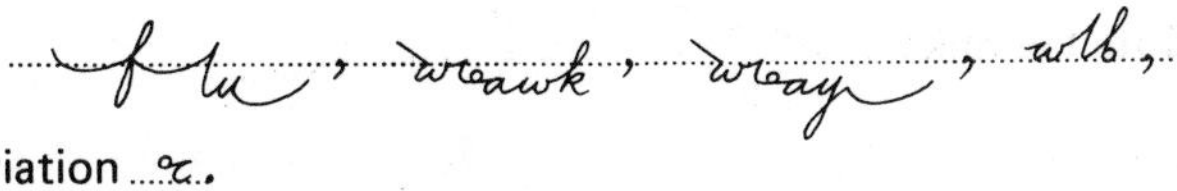

and the abbreviation 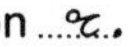

39

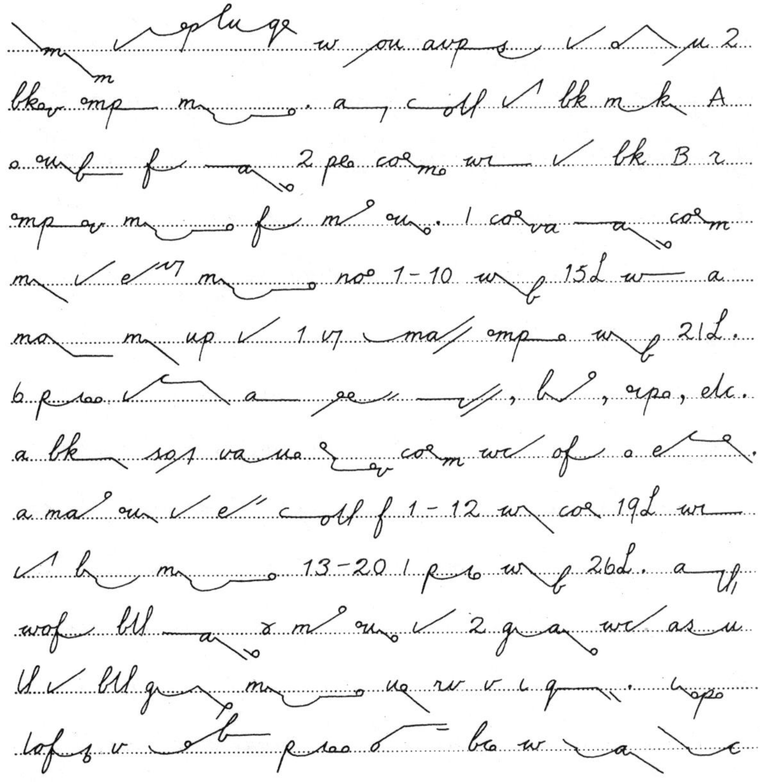

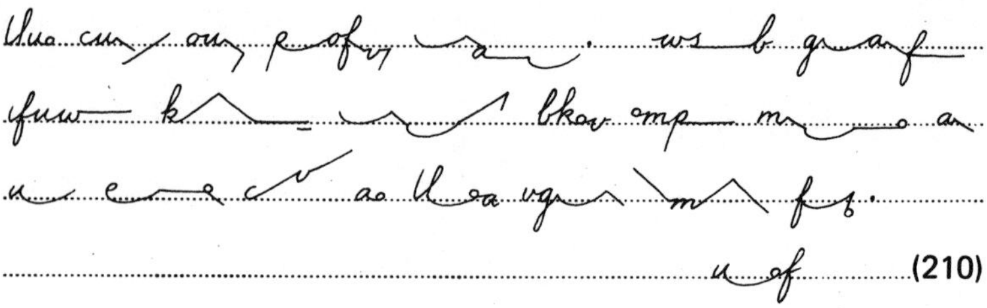

(210)

Pitman Examinations Institute

Note the links 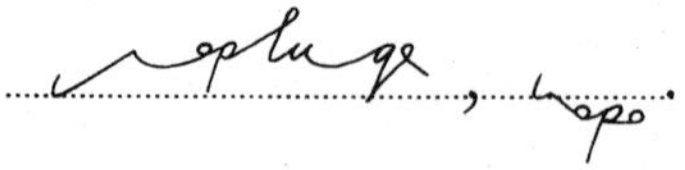

40

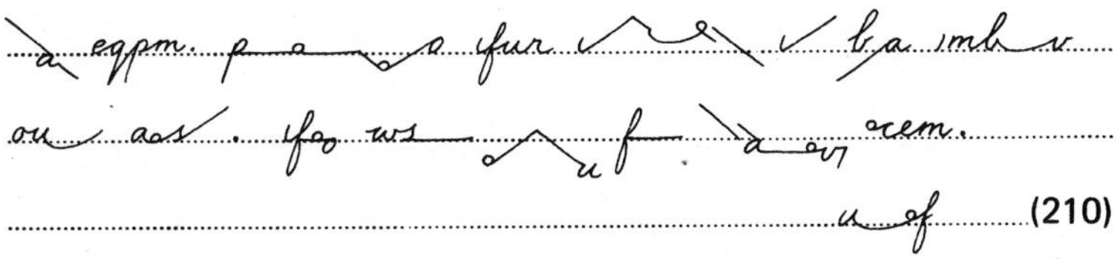

(210)

Pitman Examinations Institute

Links: 

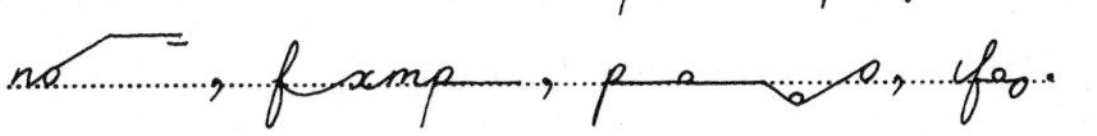 The vowel is not shown in  when repeated, and  is adequate when the word occurs more than once.

41

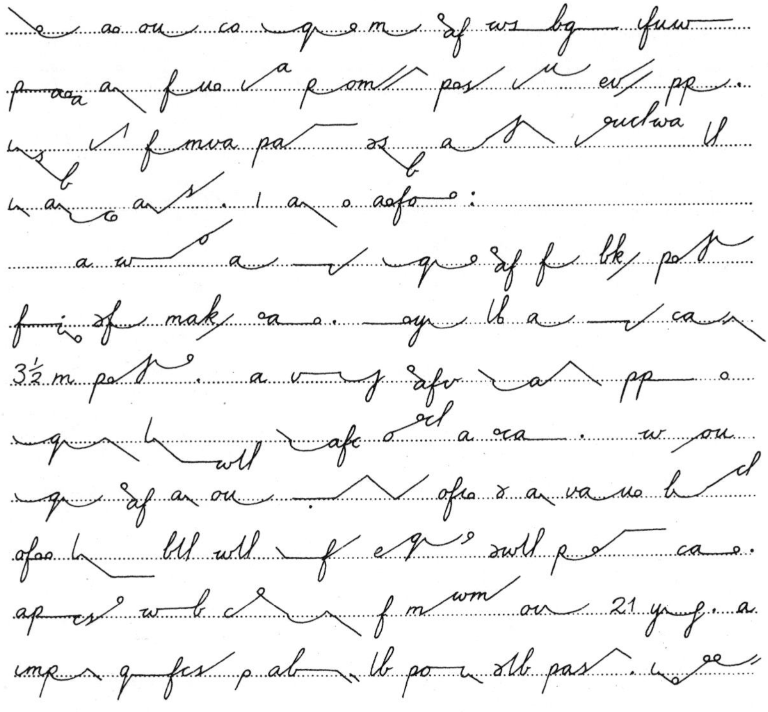

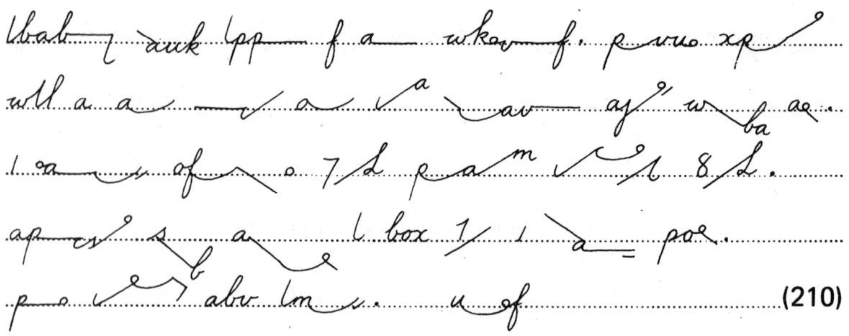

(210)

Pitman Examinations Institute

Links: 

42

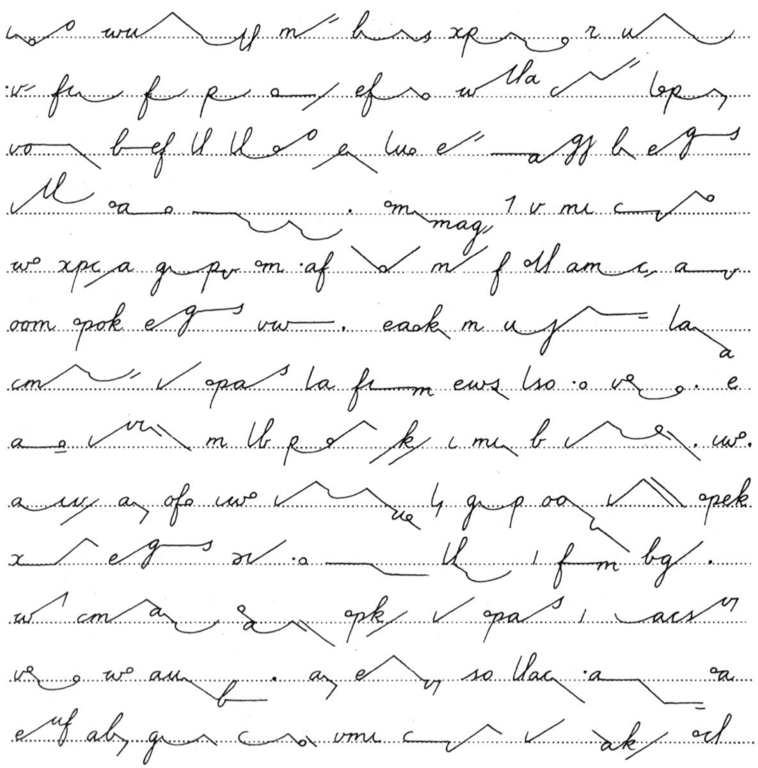

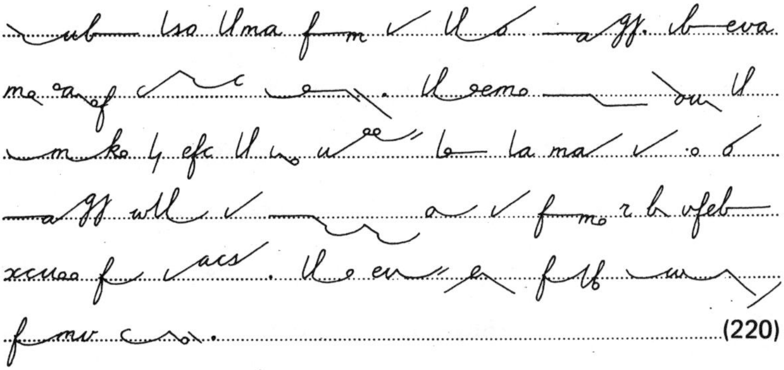

(220)

Royal Society of Arts

Dot H is omitted in *he* when the context is clear.

43

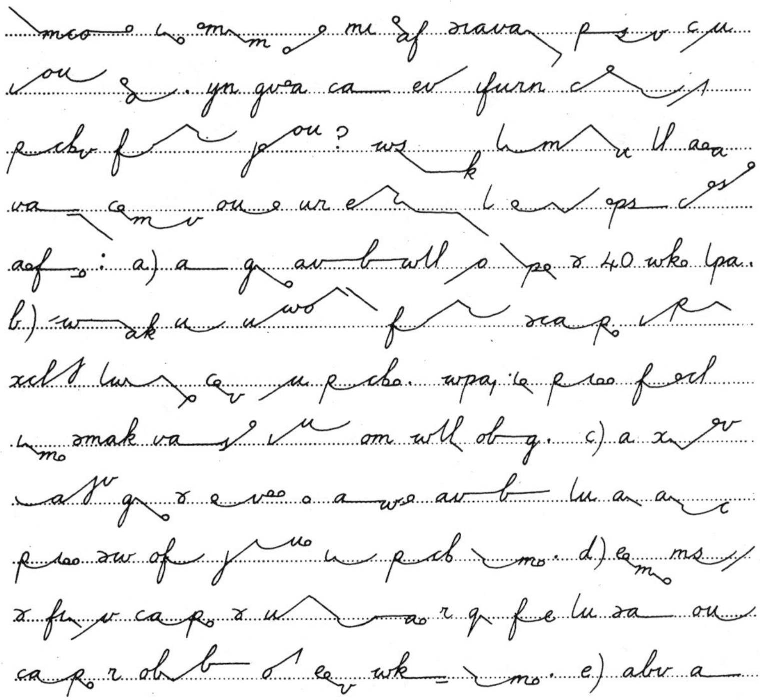

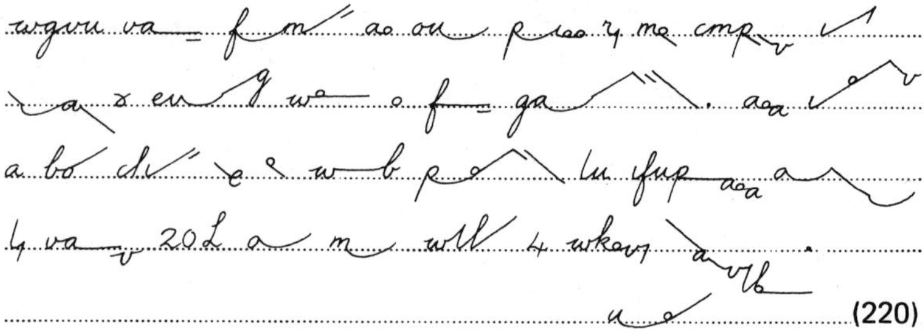

(220)

Royal Society of Arts

Links: is cut to as context is sufficient. The final a is used in but the dash is allowable here.

44

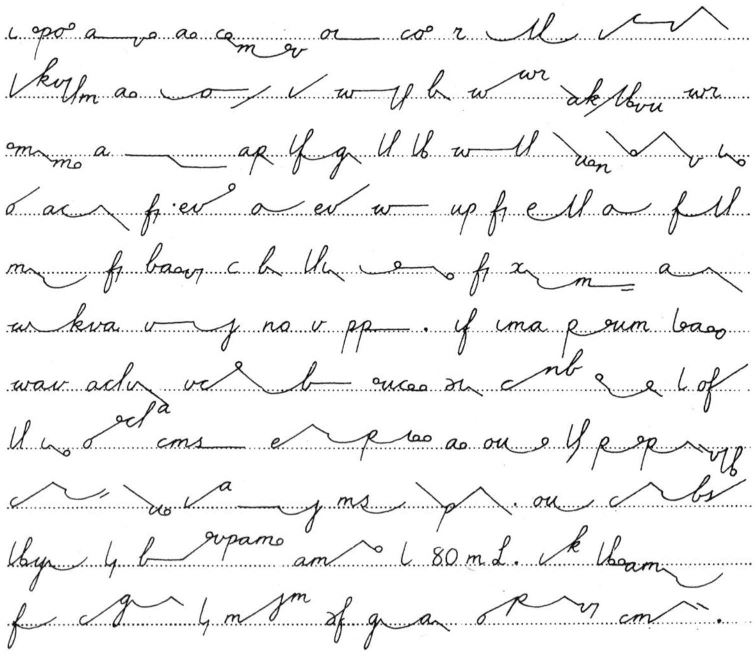

(220)

Royal Society of Arts

Links: 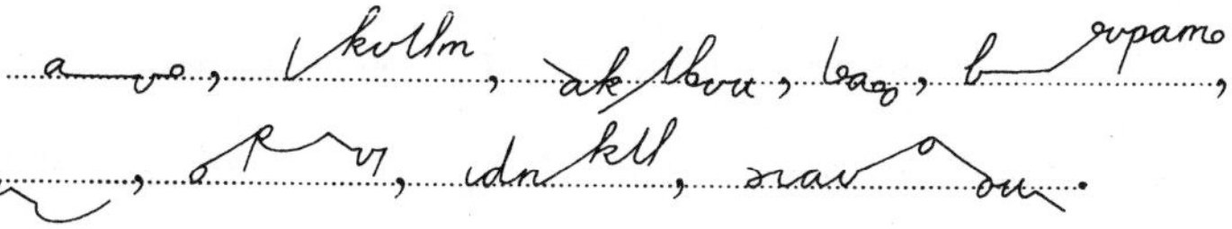

Short-cuts: 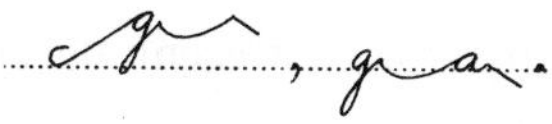

45

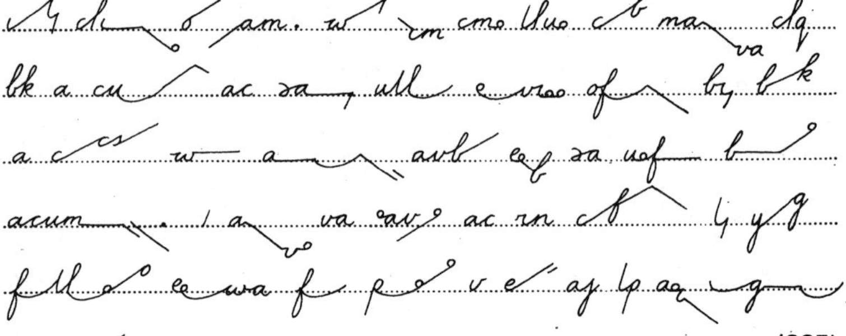

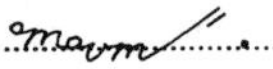 (225)

Yorkshire Council for Further Education

Vowel Omission: This is seen in 

 where consonants are sufficient indication.

After repetition, 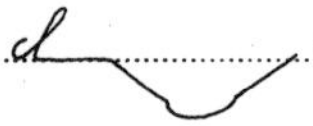 can become  and 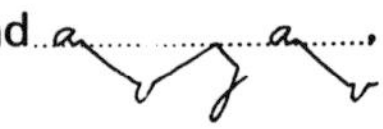

46

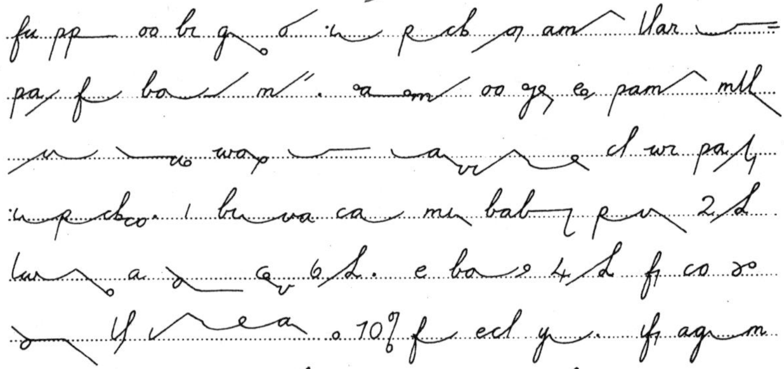

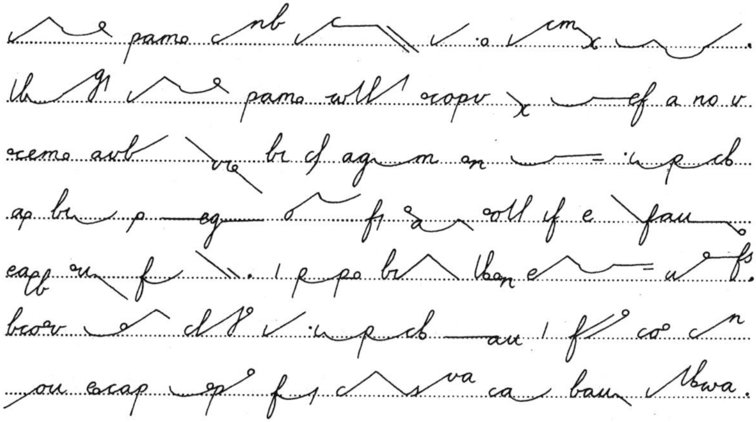

(240)

Yorkshire Council for Further Education

Note  and 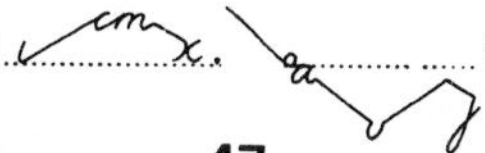 is abbreviated to 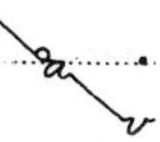.

47

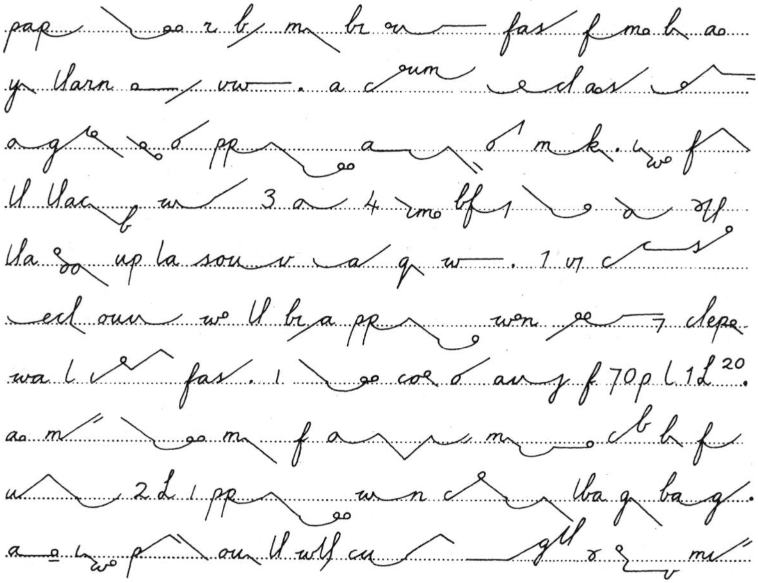

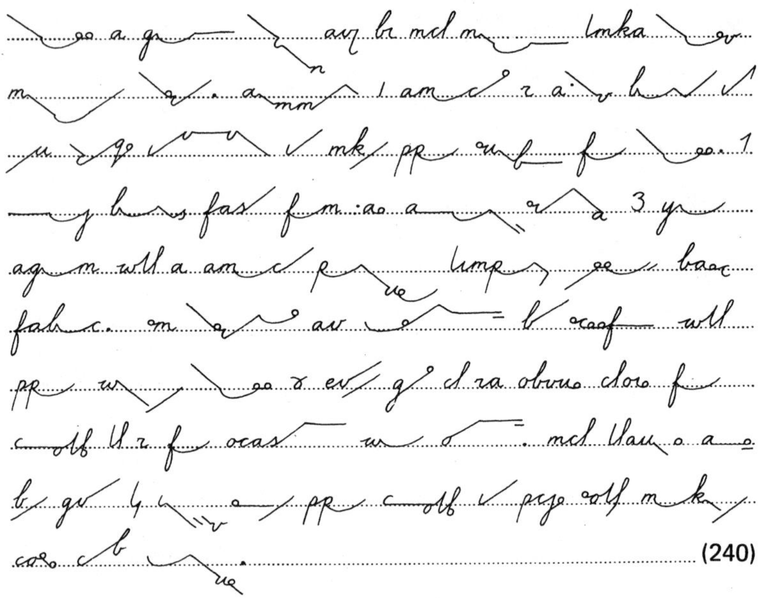

(240)

Yorkshire Council for Further Education

Paper dresses is written fully on the first occurrence and then linked.

Notice the use of m for *-ment.*

48

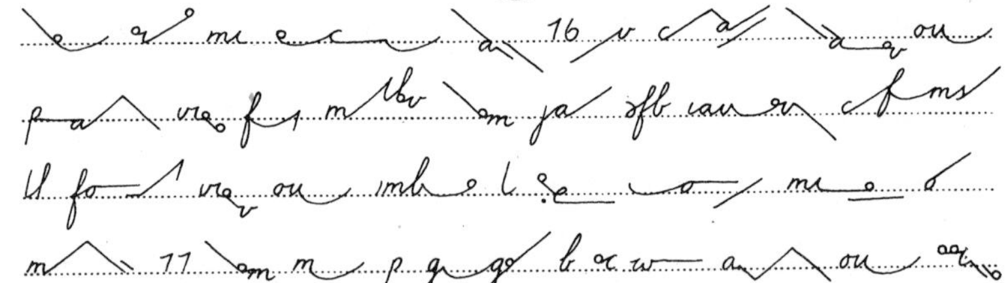

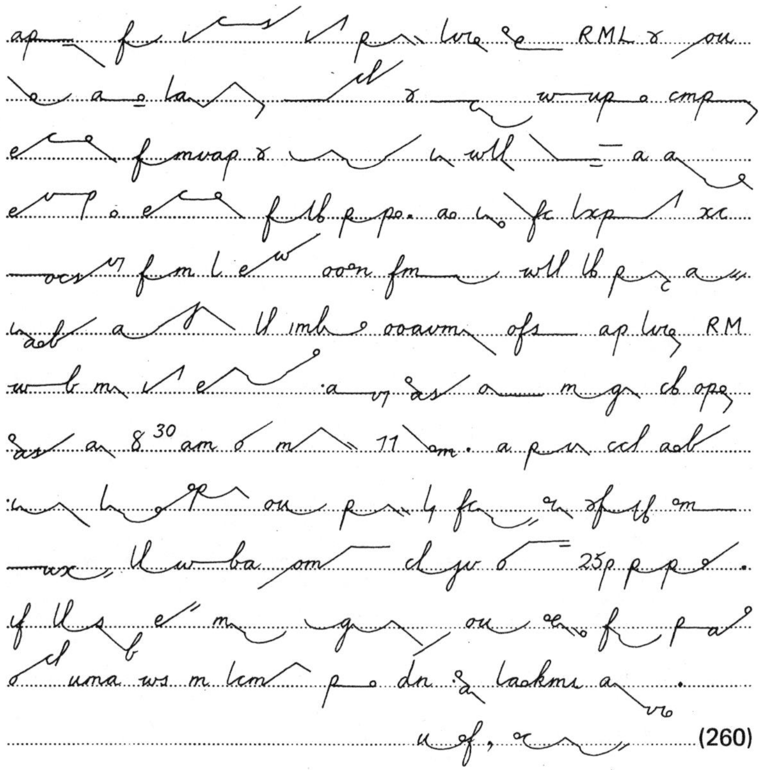

(260)

Royal Society of Arts

Points of interest are the use of RML for *Rolling Mills Ltd.*, and RM for *Rolling Mills* after the first occurrence. Note also f mvap and ap.

49

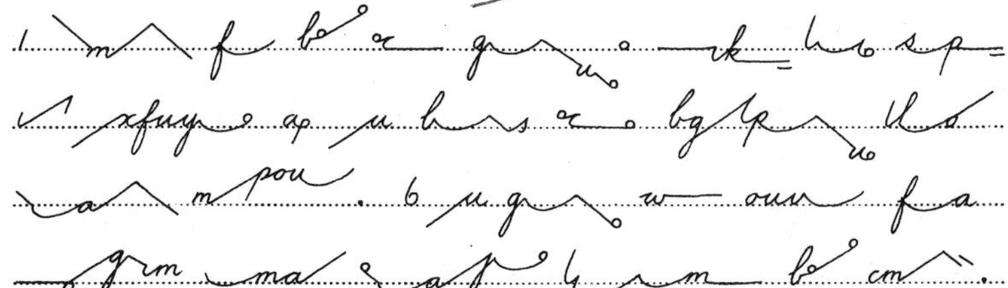

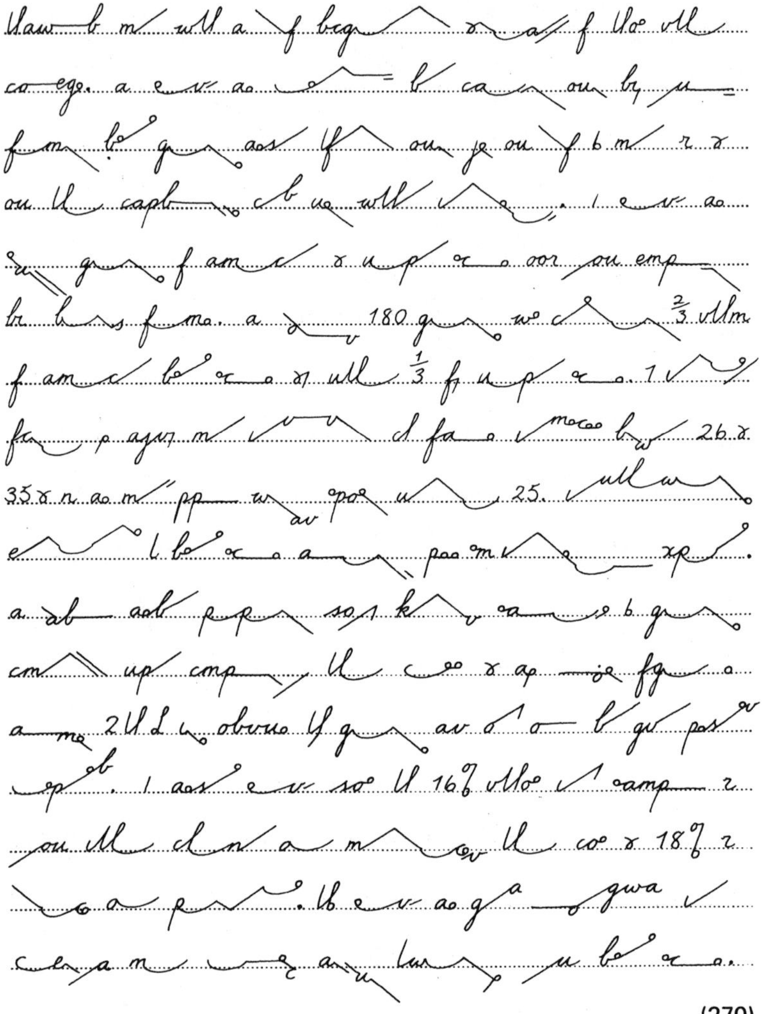

(270)

Yorkshire Council for Further Education

Links: 

Graduate is cut to  when repeated.

50

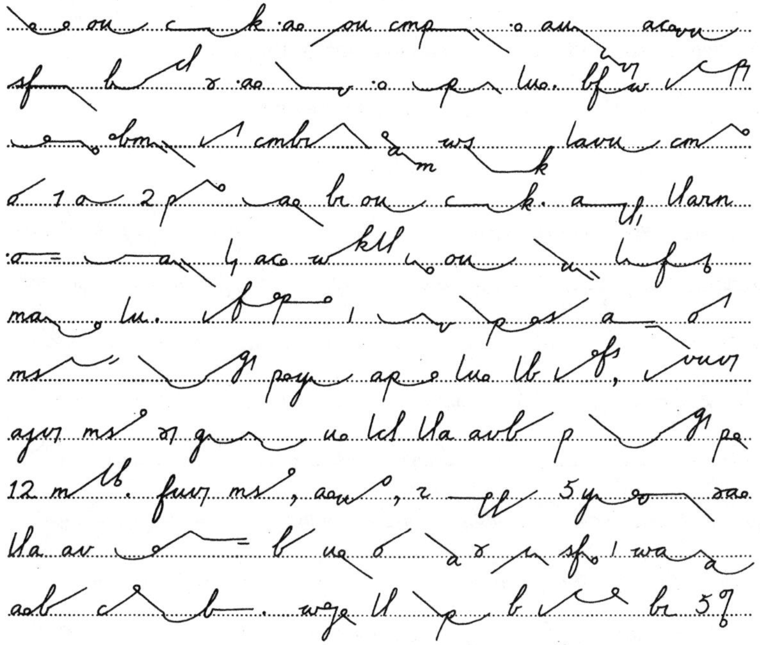

(273)

Union of Lancashire and Cheshire Institutes

Links used are …, …, …, ….

Notice … and …. Abbreviated outlines are …, …, …; and … when repeated.

51

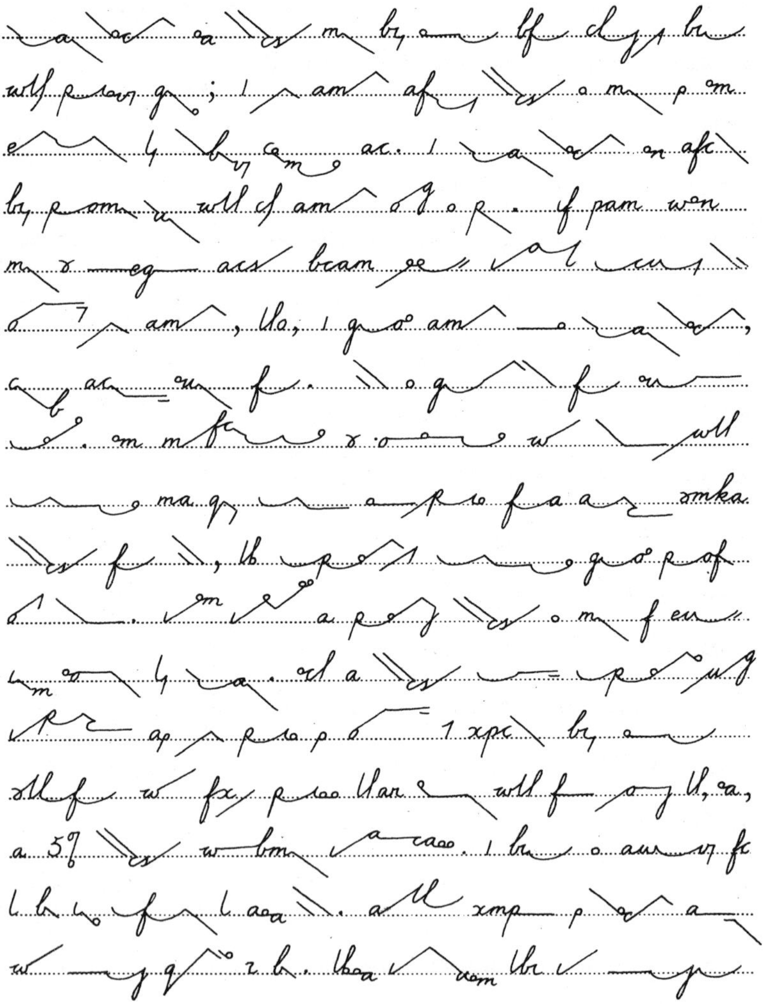

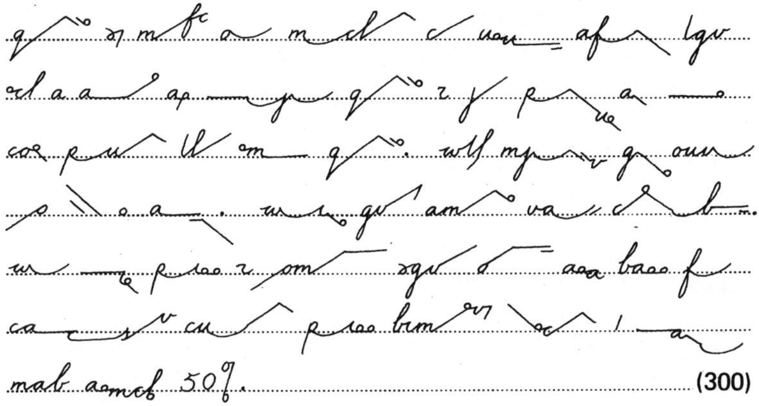

(300)

London Chamber of Commerce

Abbreviations to note are . Some useful links are  for  when it occurs repeatedly, and .

52

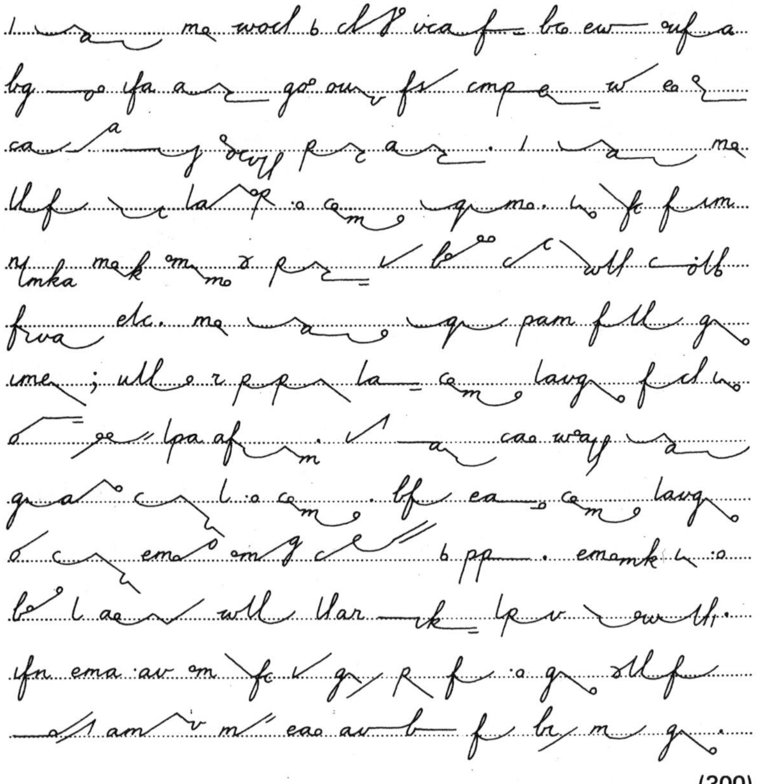

(300)

London Chamber of Commerce

Some links are 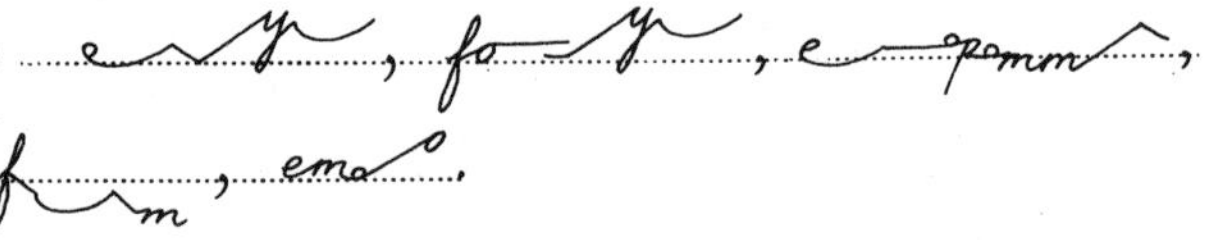

53

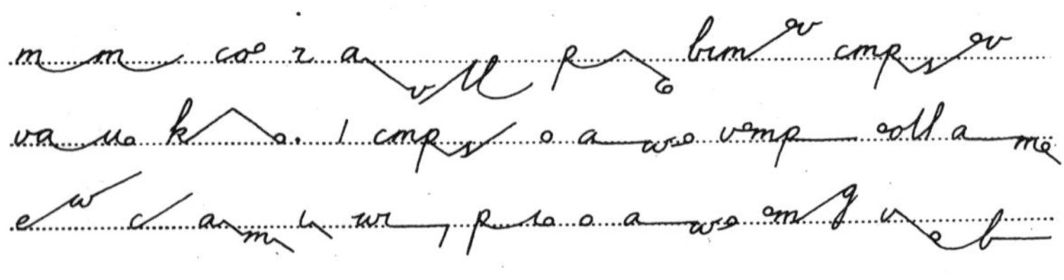

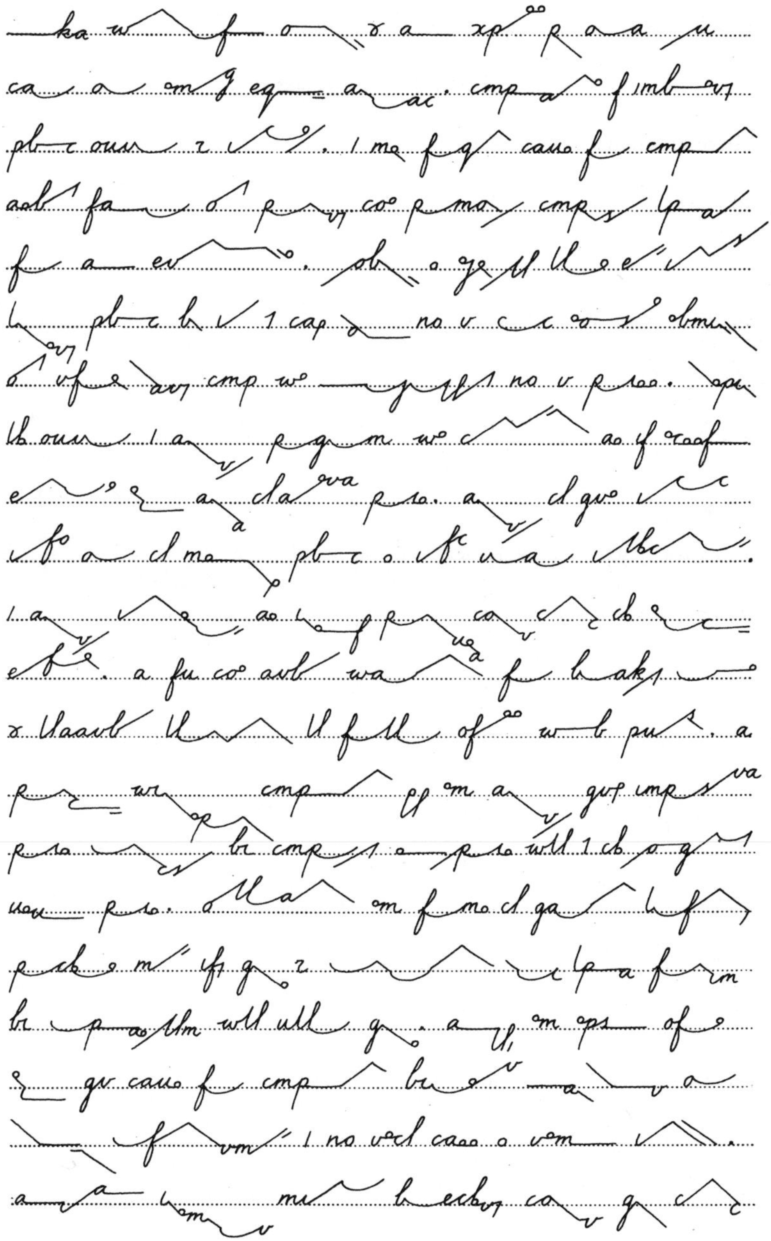

 (300)

Royal Society of Arts

There are many instances of vowel omission in this passage. Links are

54

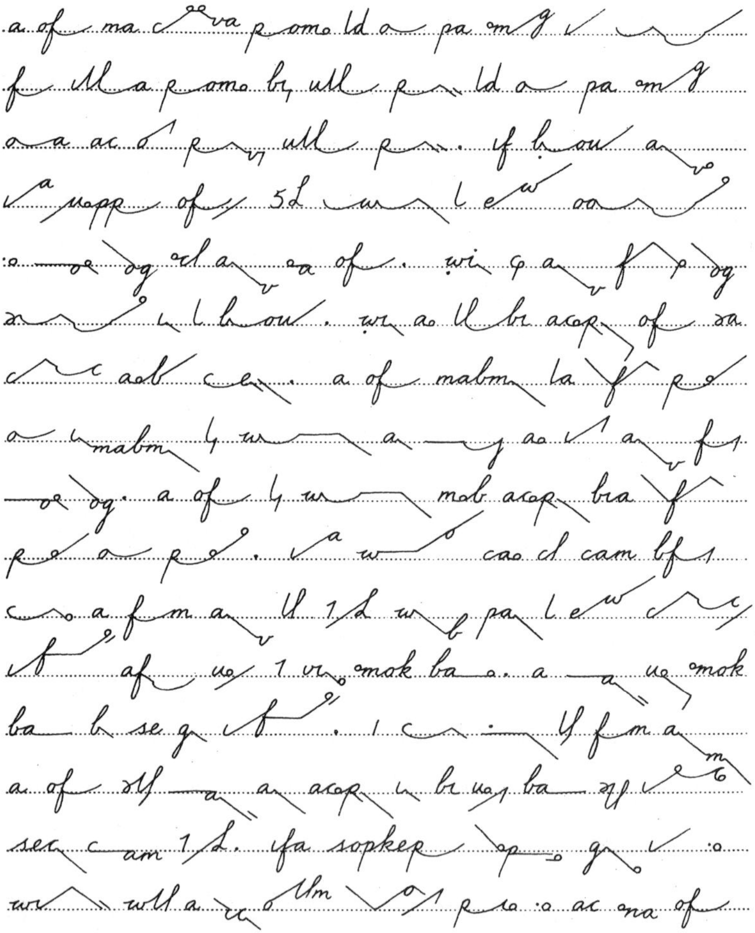

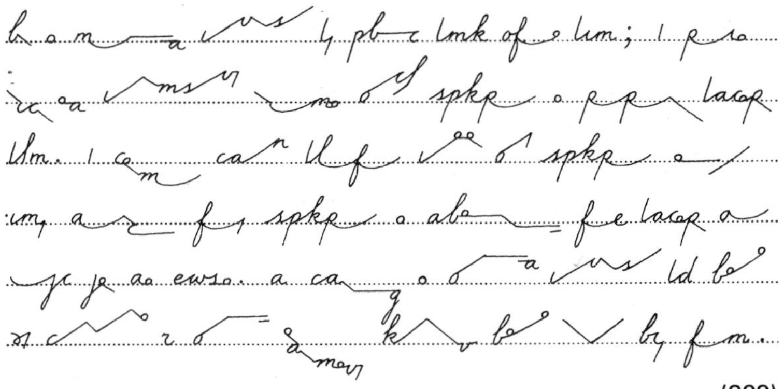

(300)

London Chamber of Commerce

___ is used for *hundred* in ___. The vowels are omitted from *shopkeeper* when the word is repeated.

55

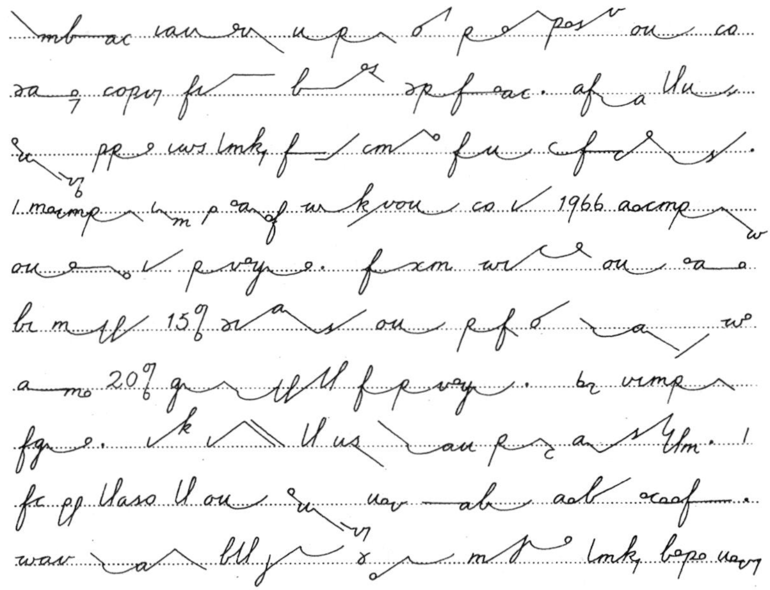

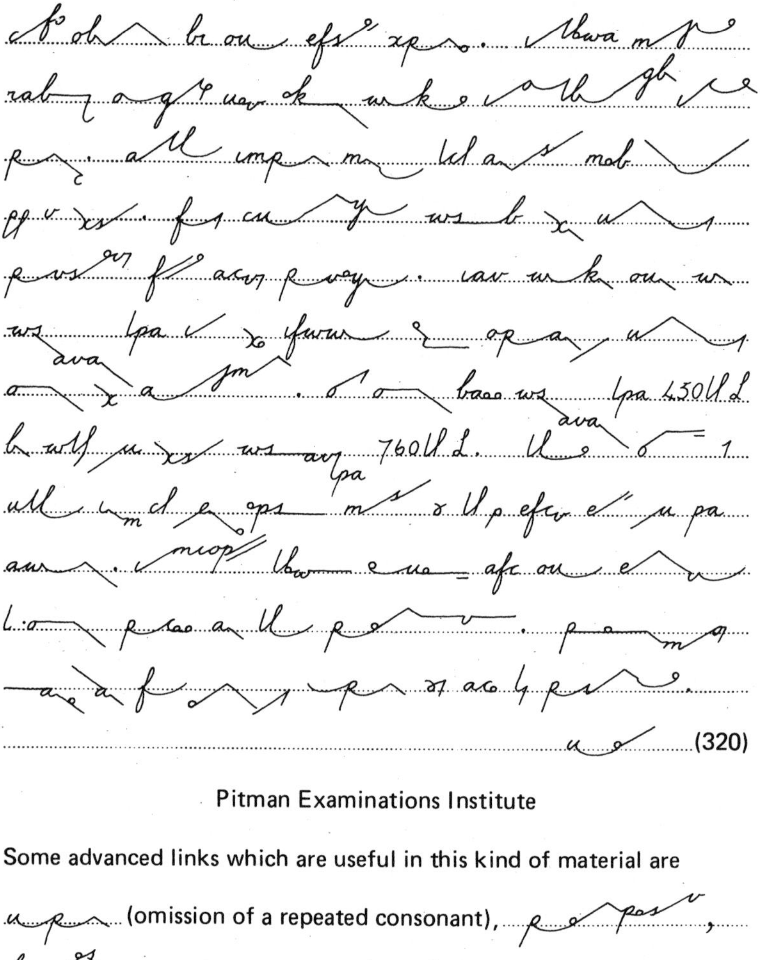

(320)

Pitman Examinations Institute

Some advanced links which are useful in this kind of material are

 (omission of a repeated consonant), 

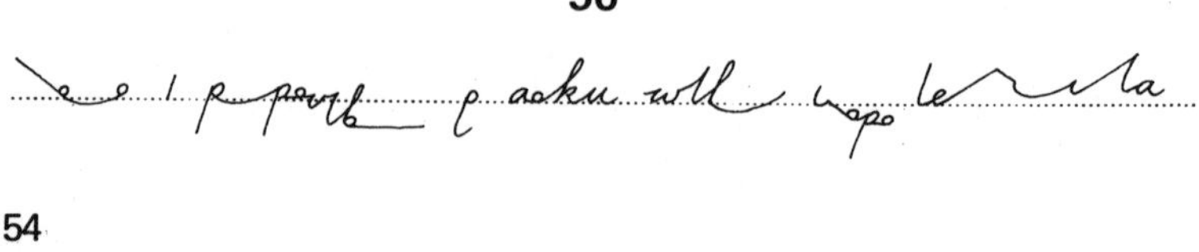

56

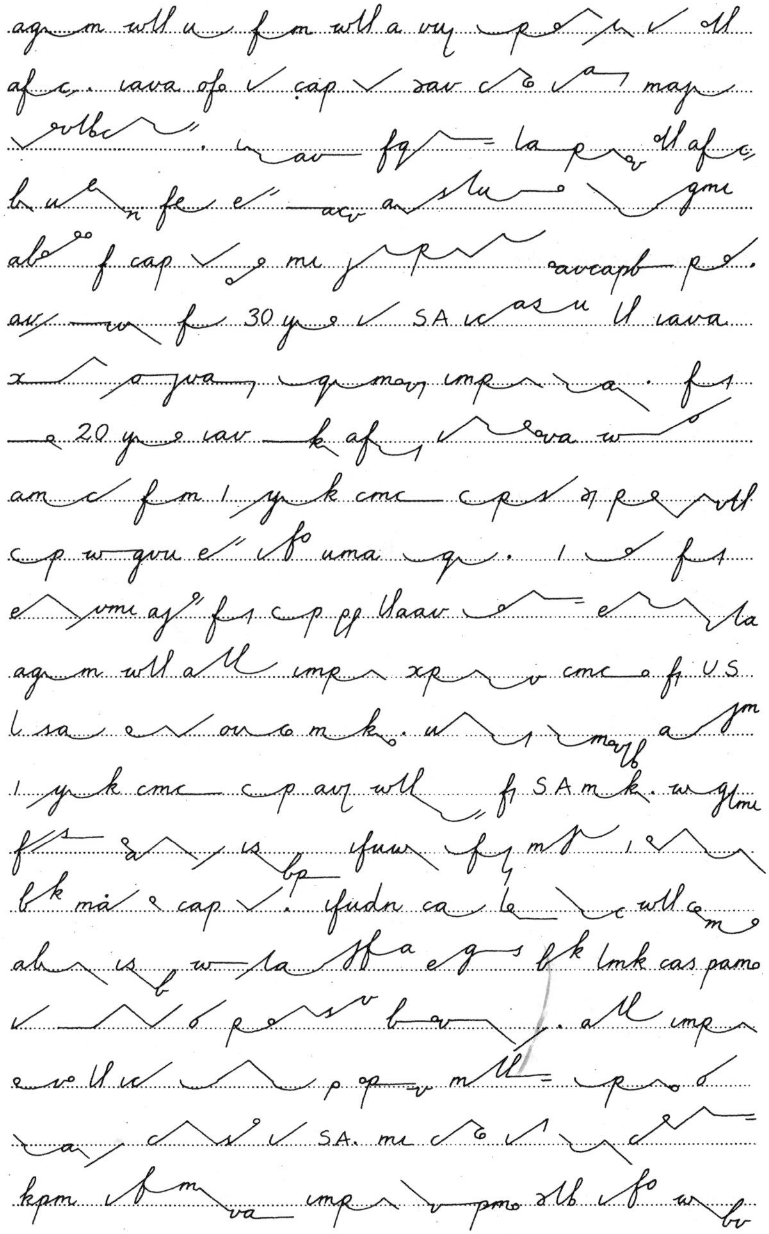

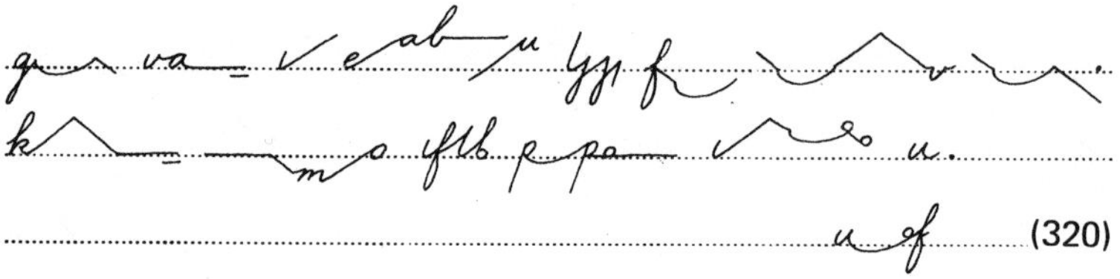

(320)

Pitman Examinations Institute

Among the many links used in this passage are

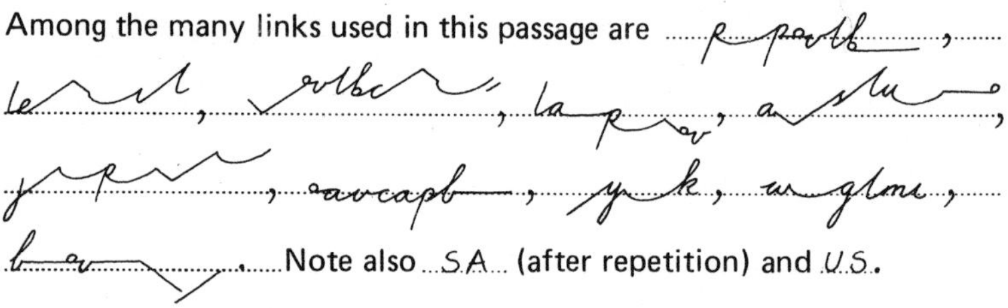

Note also S.A. (after repetition) and U.S.

 can be cut to  when repeated.

57

(321)

Union of Lancashire and Cheshire Institutes

m is used for *million* in *150m*. *Establishment* is cut to *ef*.

58

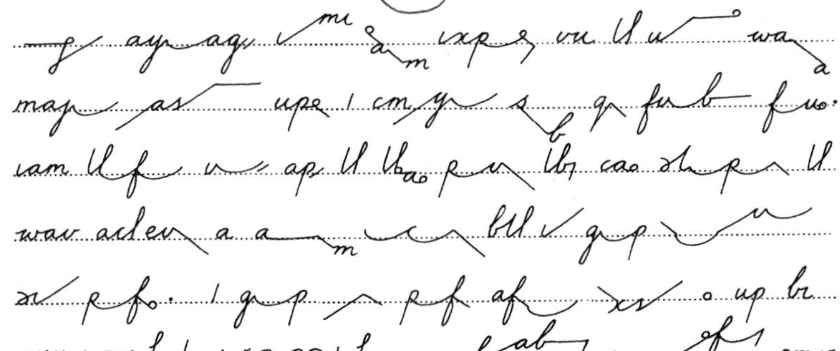

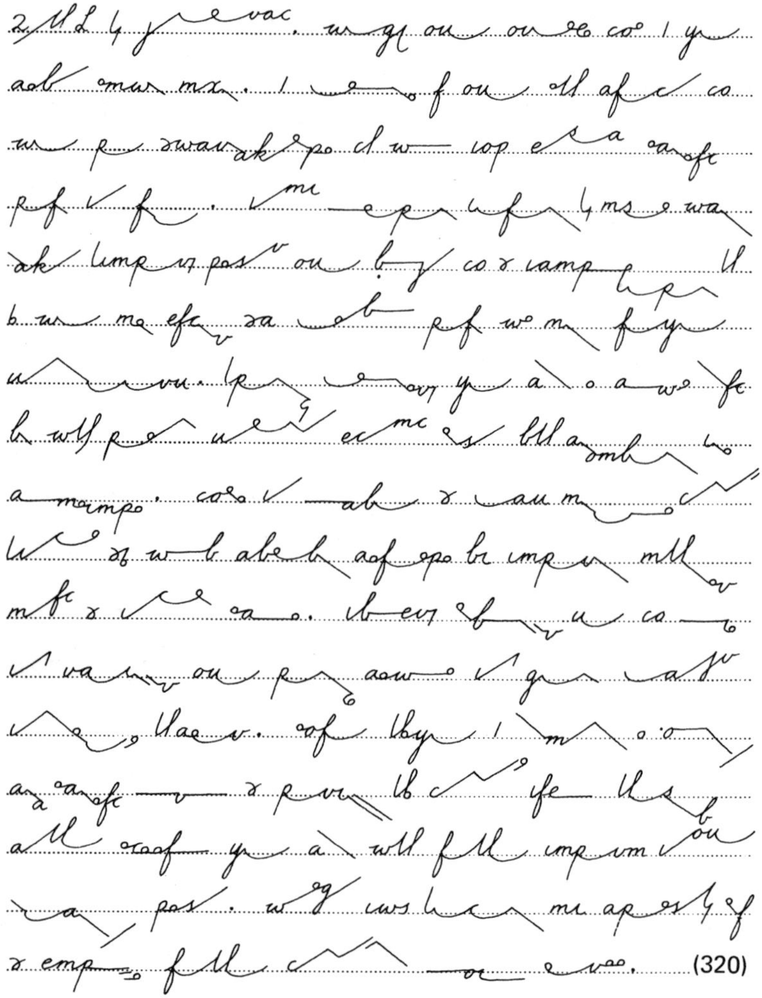

(320)

East Midland Educational Union

Links worth noting are 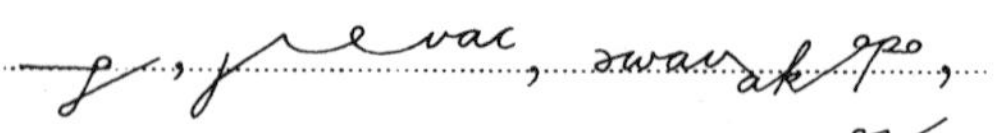

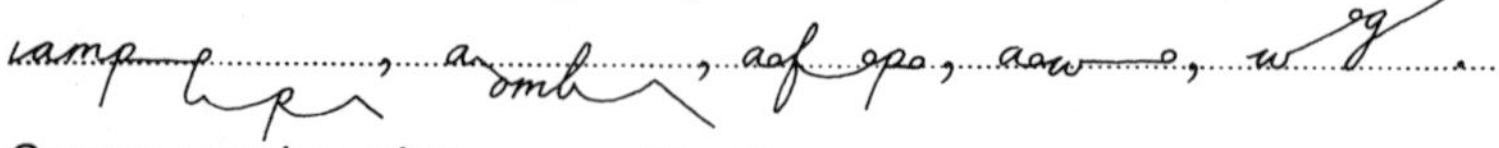

Overseas can be written  or 

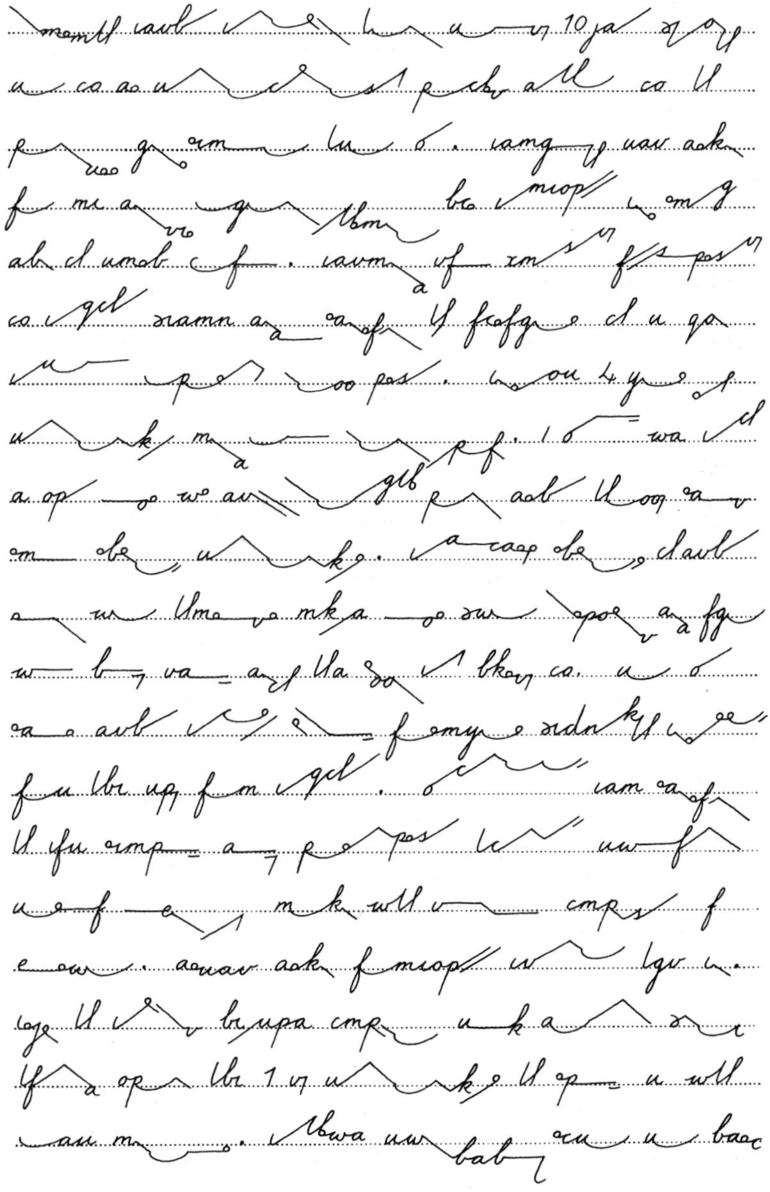

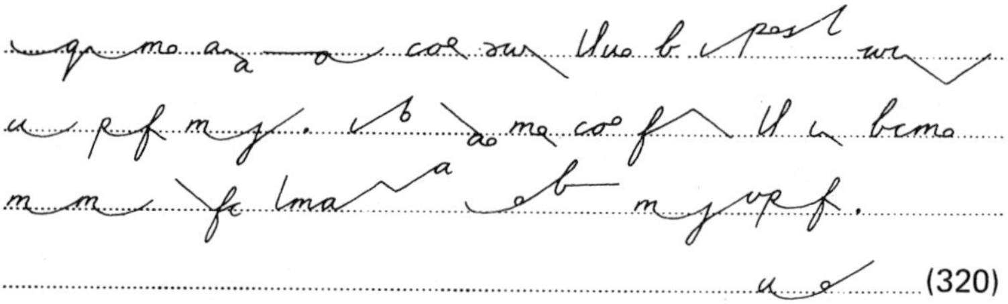

(320)

Pitman Examinations Institute

Several examples of vowel omission are seen in this passage.

 is a useful link to memorize.

60

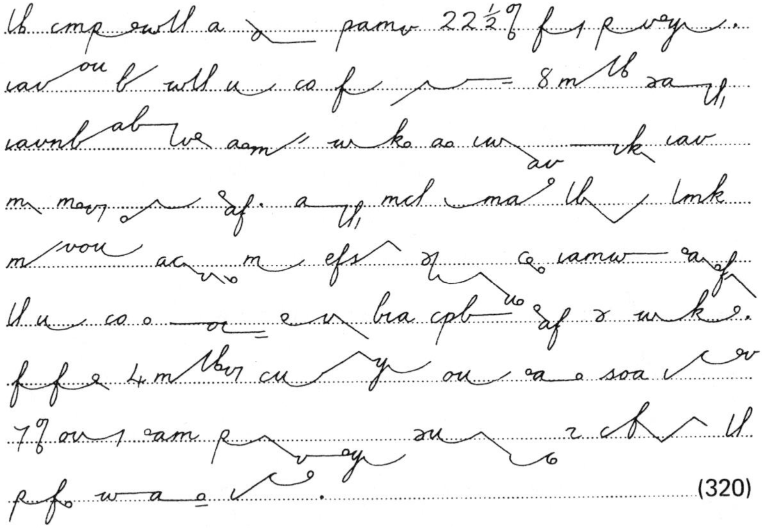

(320)

East Midland Educational Union

This passage offers many opportunities for linking, and examples are

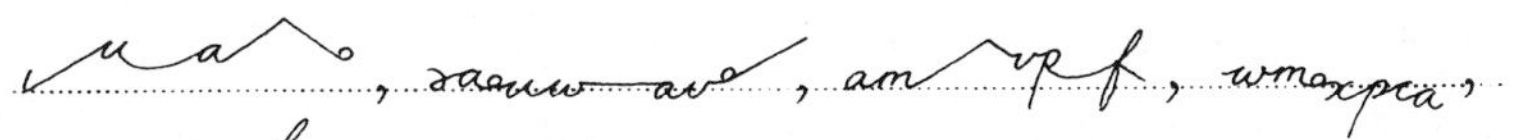

 Notice 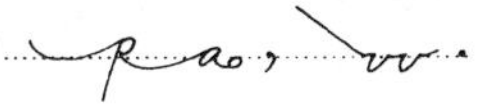

61

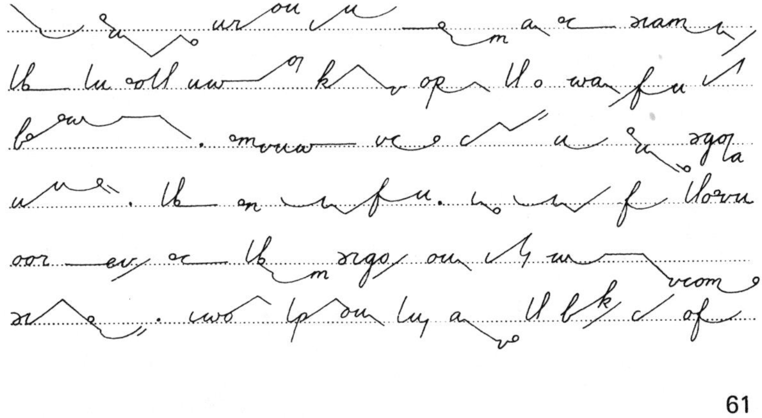

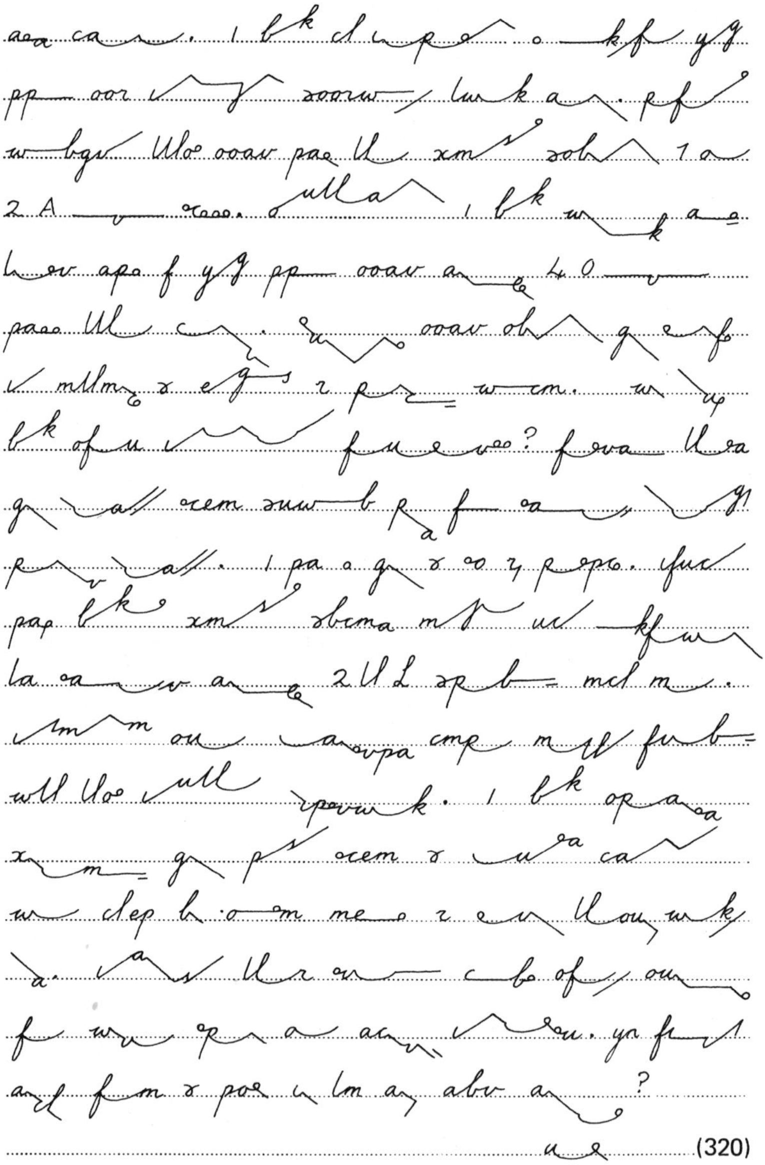

(320)

Pitman Examinations Institute

62

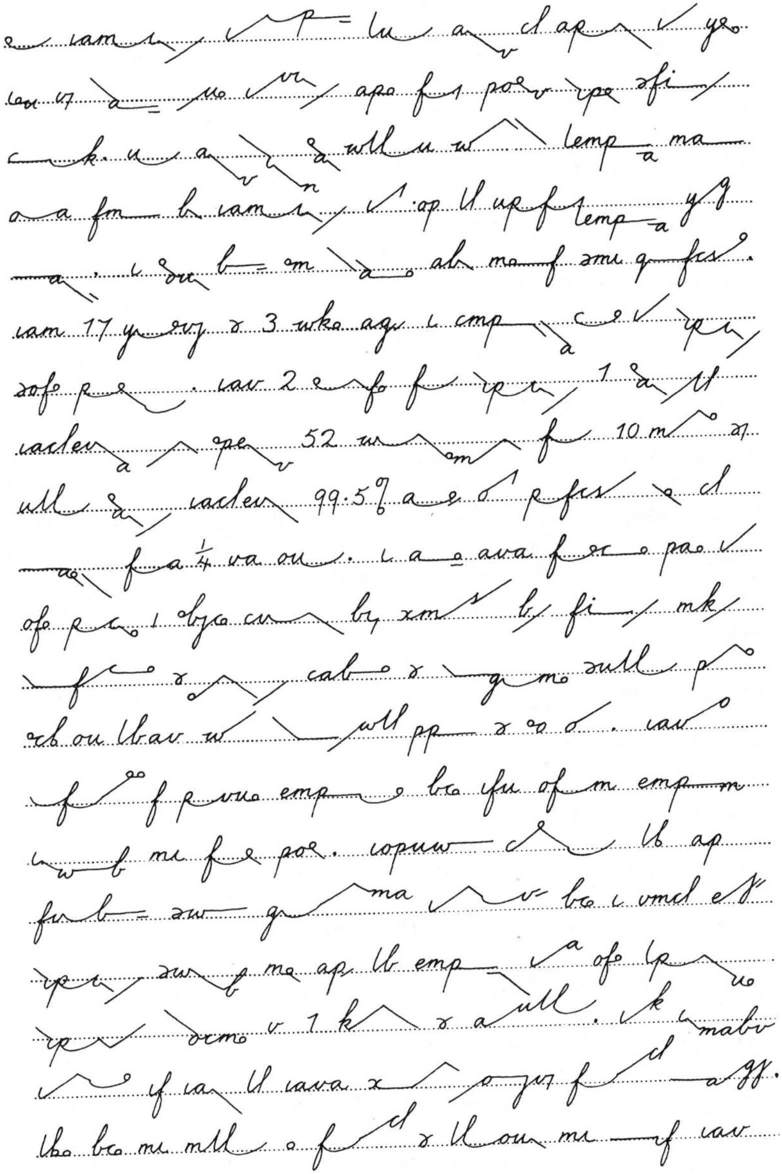

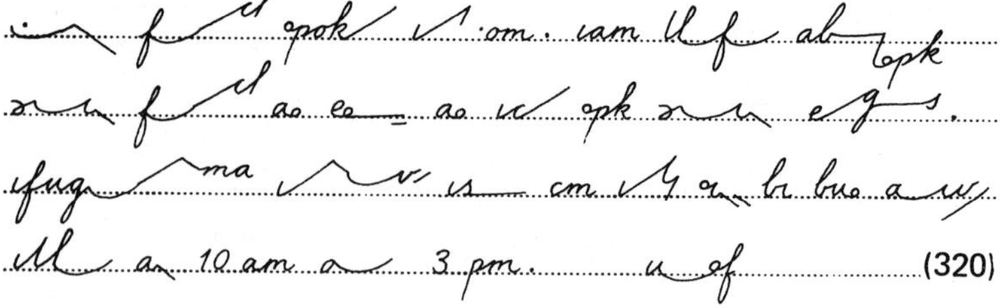

(320)

Pitman Examinations Institute

Note  and 

63

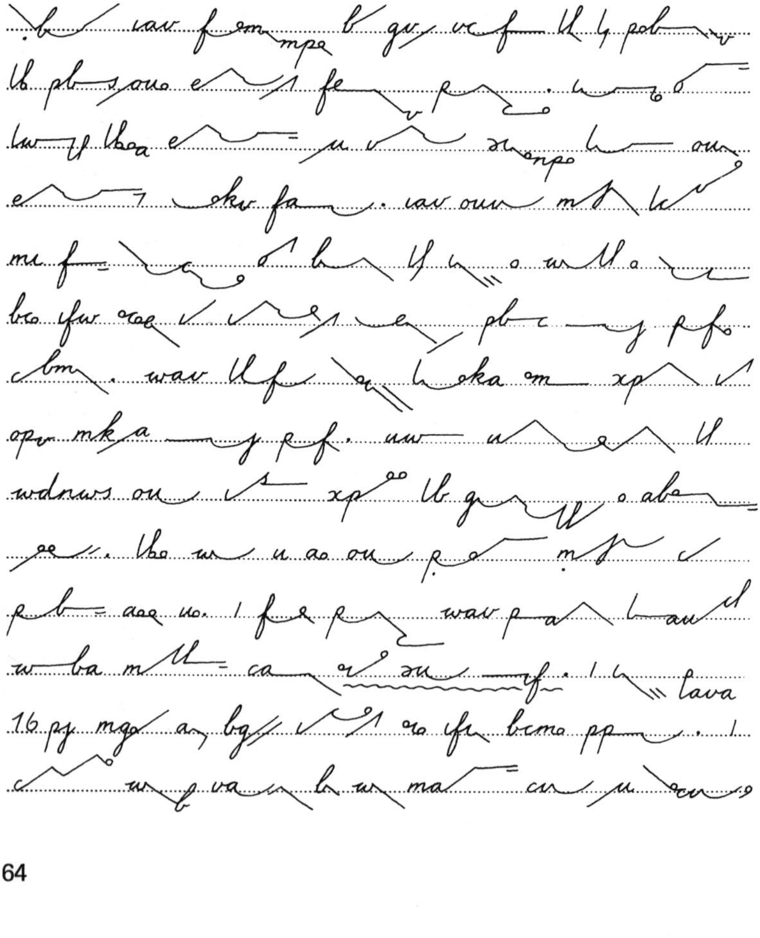

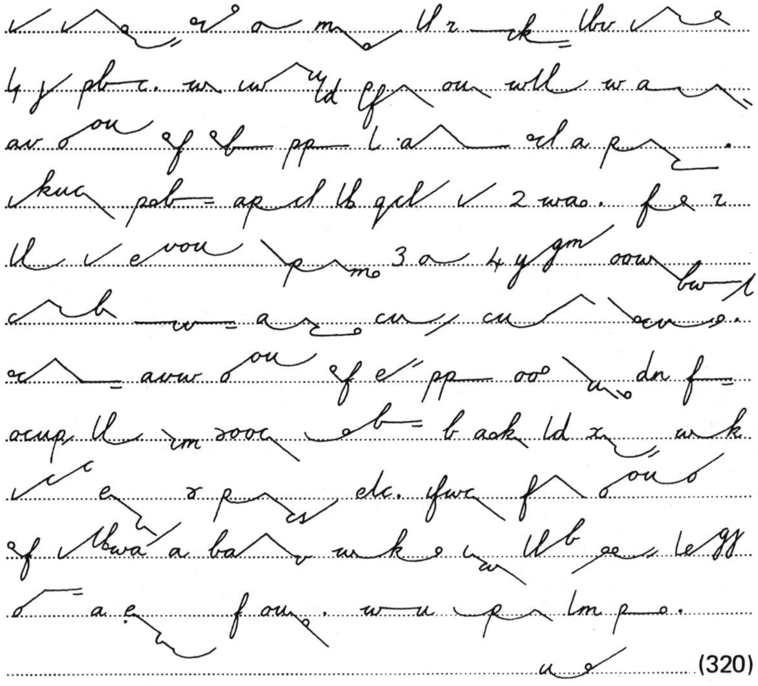

(320)

Pitman Examinations Institute

There are abundant examples of vowel omission in this passage to study and imitate. *With* is omitted in  for *in connection with*. Note

64

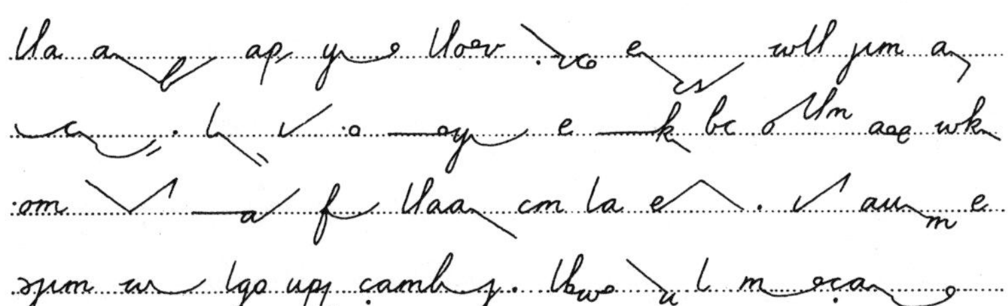

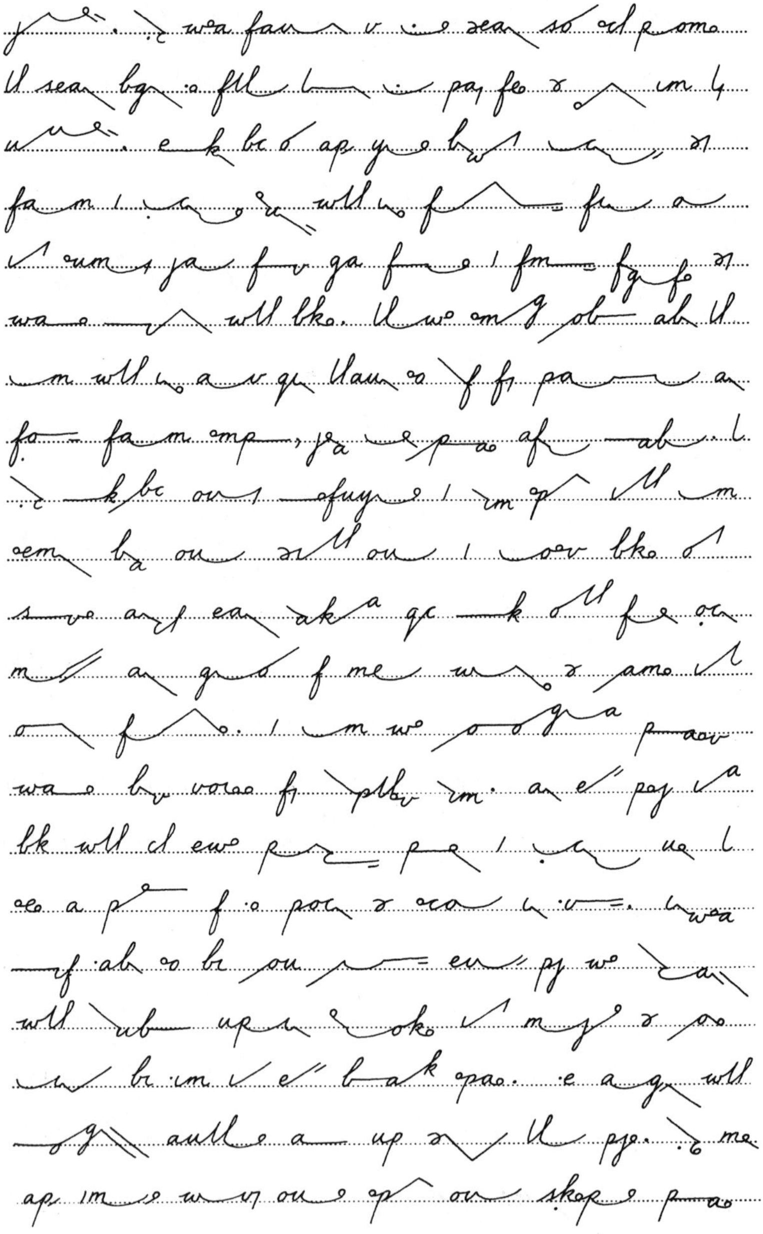

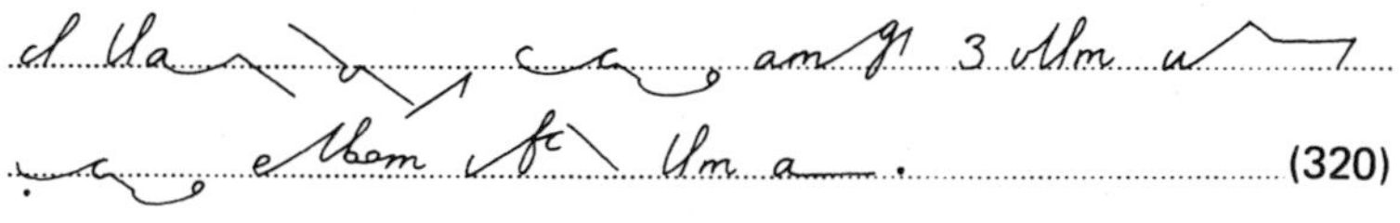

(320)

East Midland Educational Union

There is no need to vocalize *Dick* after the first occurrence. Simple words such as *back* and *walked* do not need a vowel in context, and the consonants are adequate in longer words like *character. H* can often safely be omitted.

65

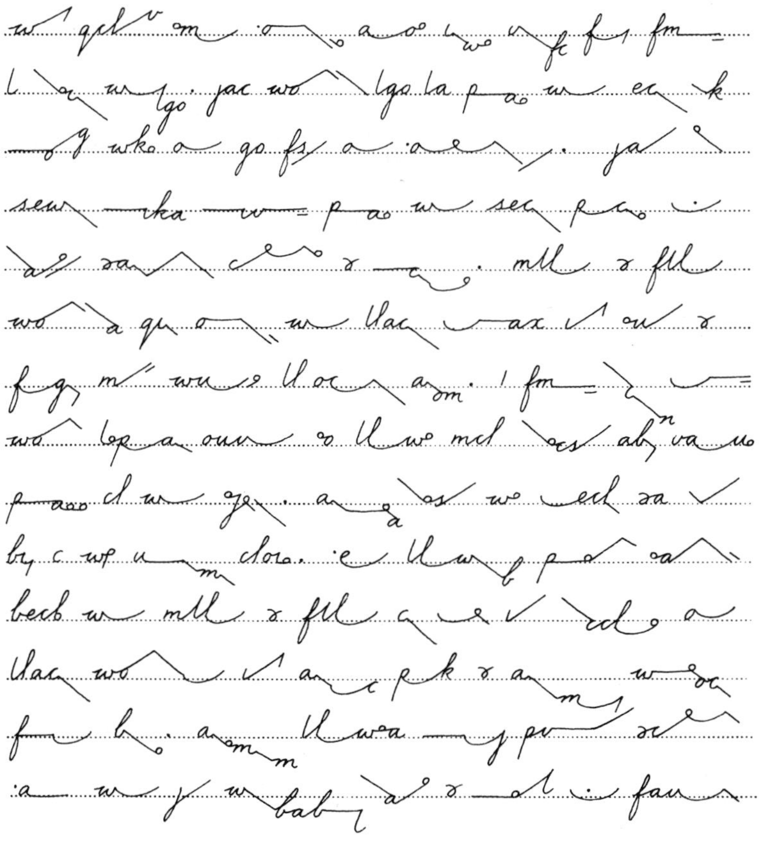

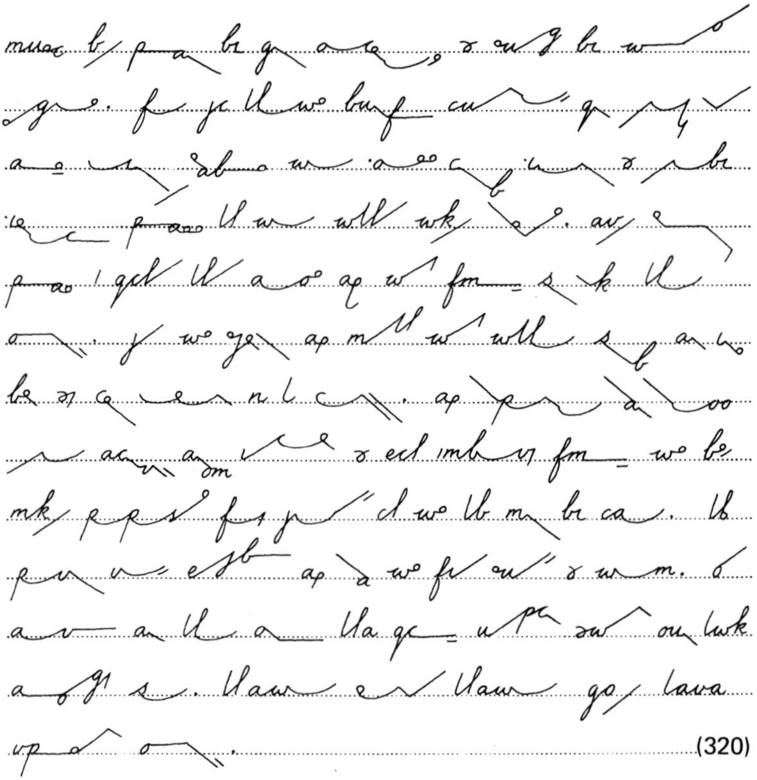

(320)

Pitman Examinations Institute

Here again names are not vocalized when repeated:  *Sea* is  but derivatives can be written either with the 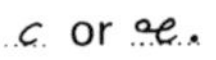 Thus *seaside* is shown as  but  would be acceptable.

66

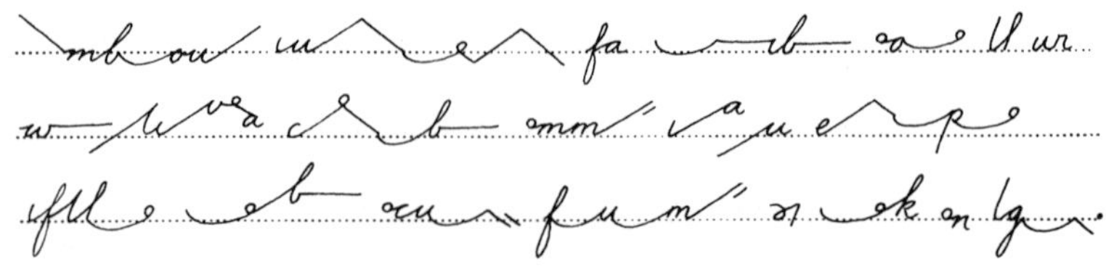

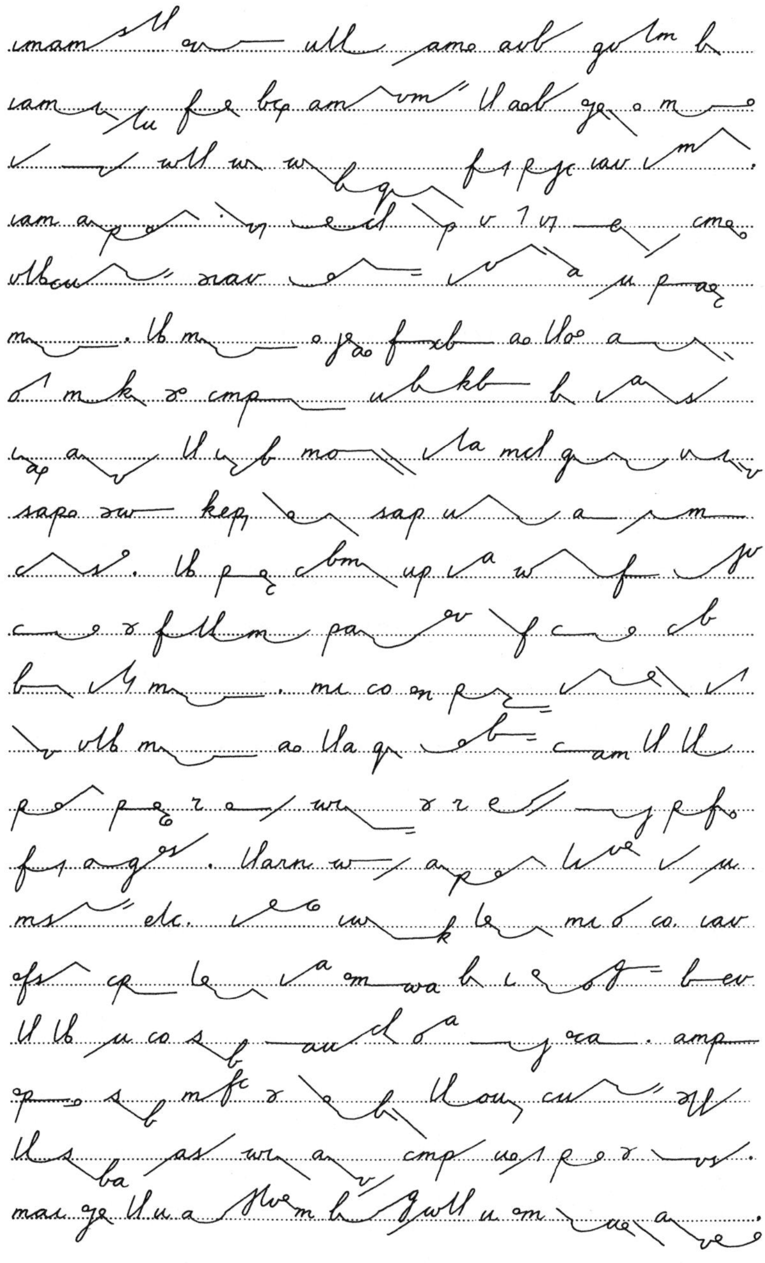

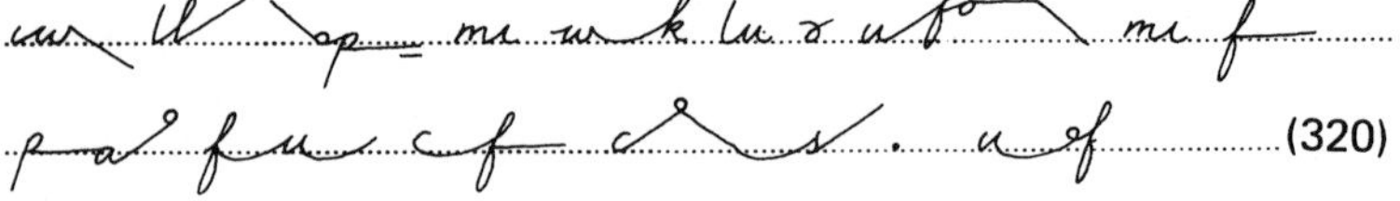 (320)

Pitman Examinations Institute

Department and *development* are cut to  and 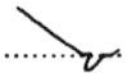 as confusion cannot arise. Note the links  – all expressions of common occurrence.

67

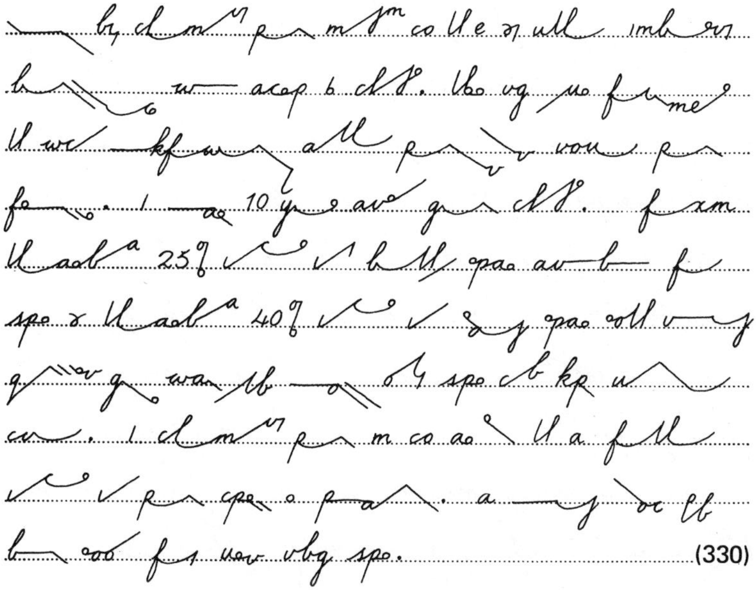

(330)

Pitman Examinations Institute

After *management* has been repeated it is finally reduced to *m.* Links worth using are  and   is suggested for *Board of Directors.*

68

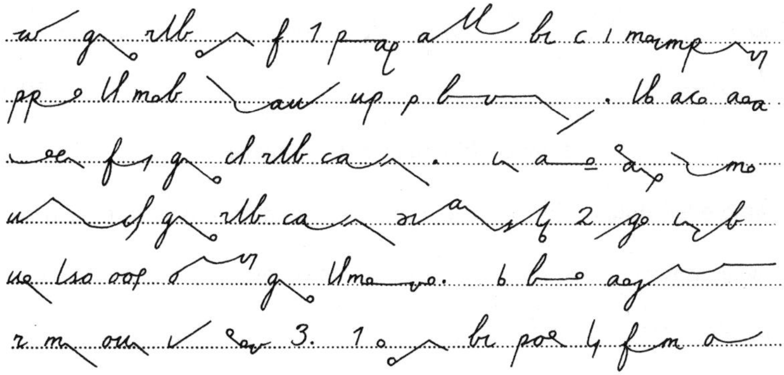

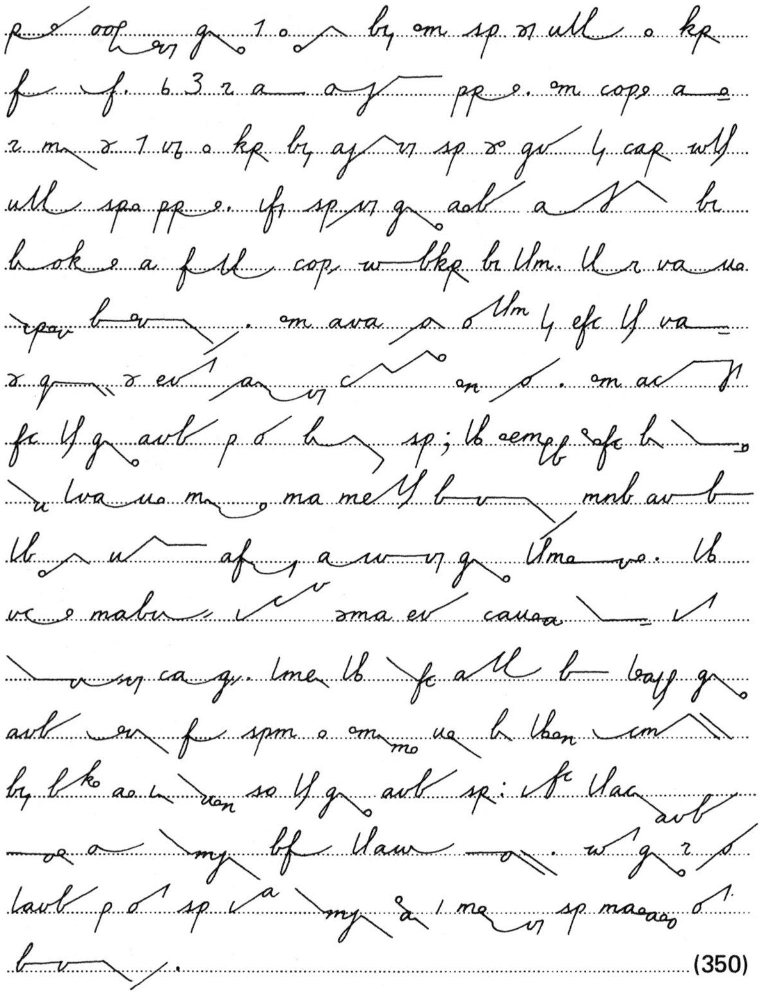

(350)

London Chamber of Commerce

Remember that 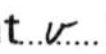 for *of* can often be joined to the tick for a final vowel, as in 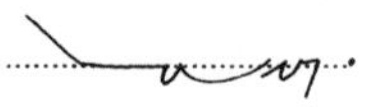. Other links are 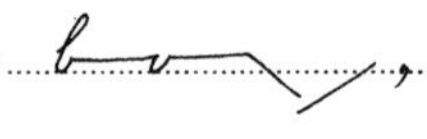, 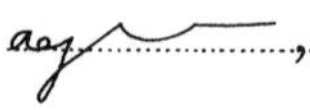, .

69

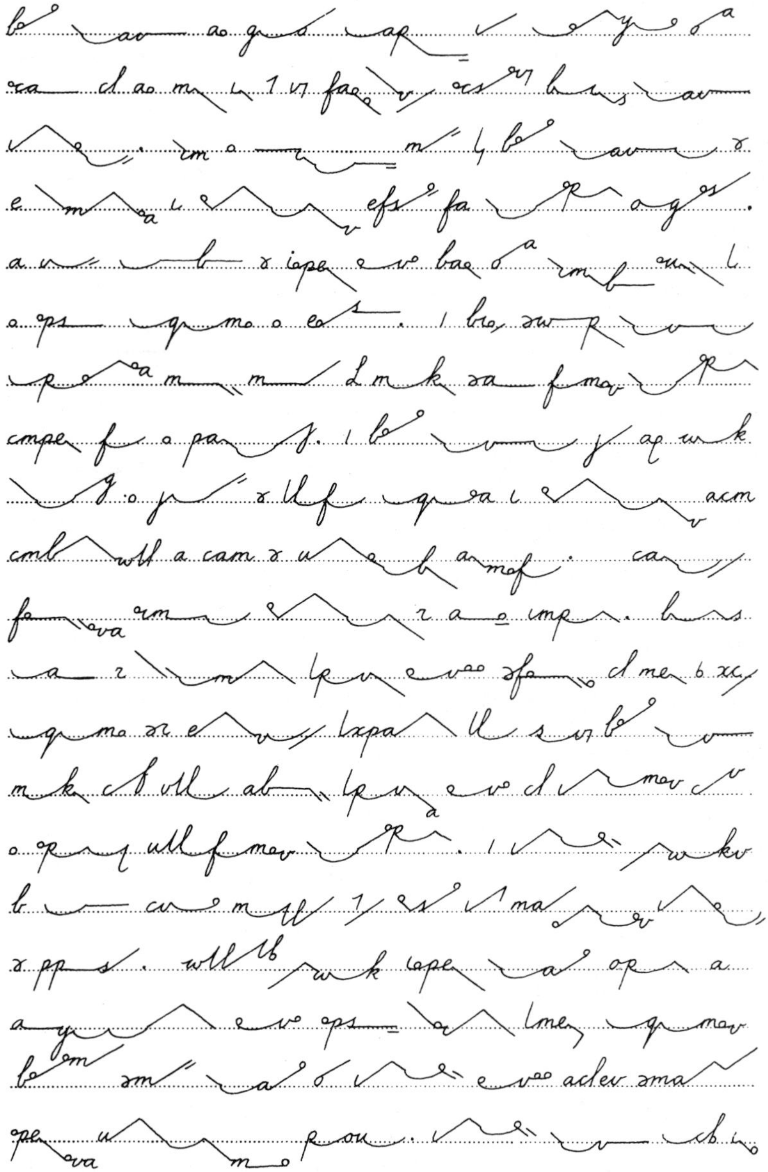

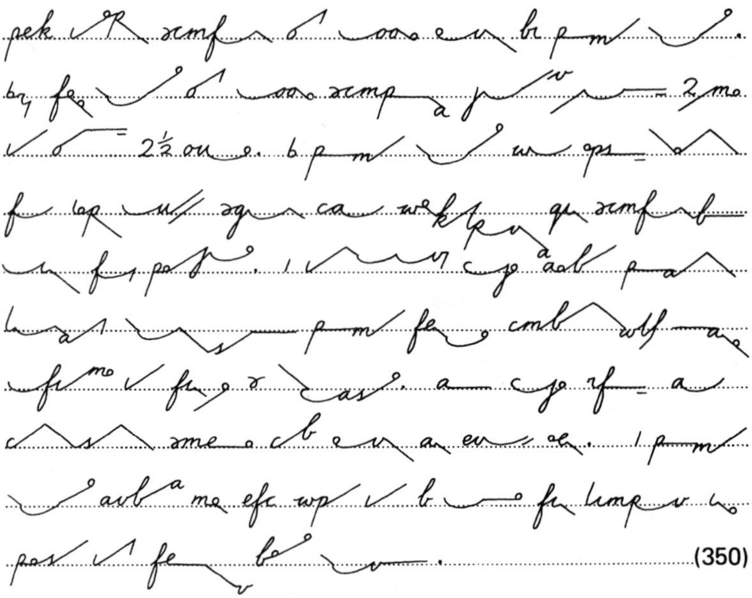

(350)

Yorkshire Council for Further Education

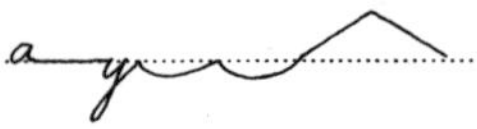 and  are two of the links which have been used. After repetition 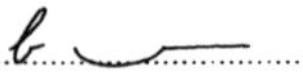 is used for *British Rail,* and many vowels are omitted in repeated words.

70

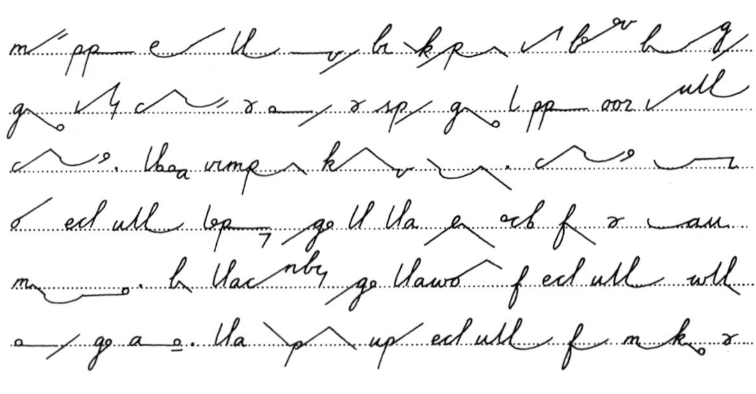

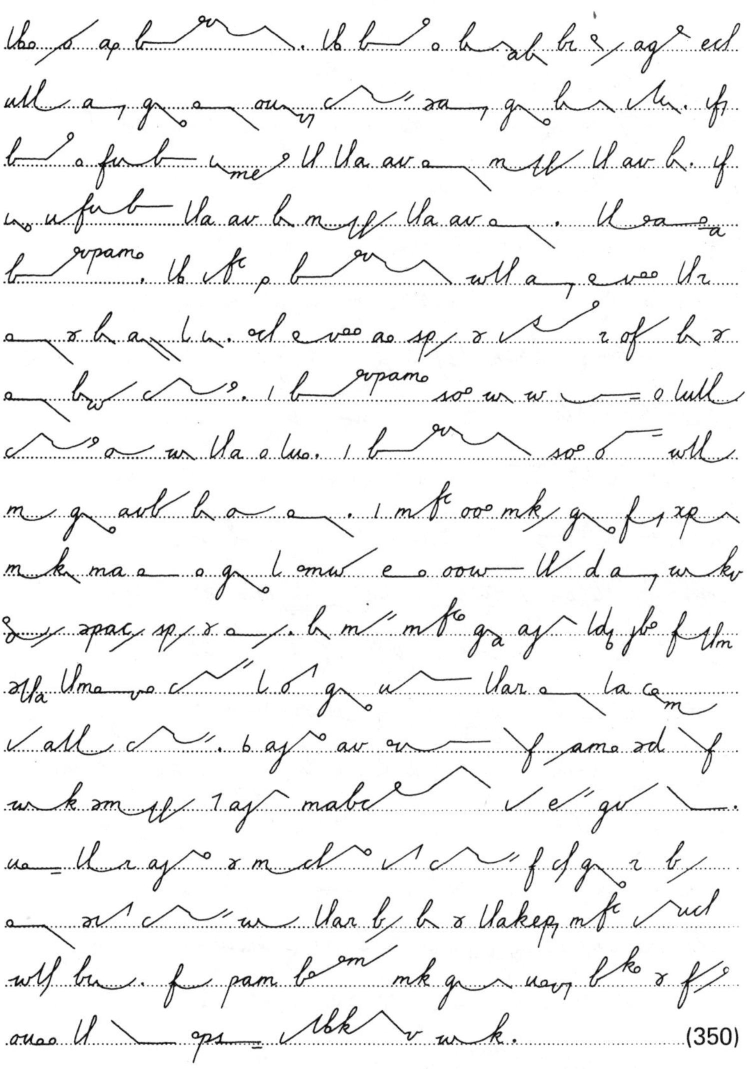

(350)

London Chamber of Commerce

An experienced writer could use  and 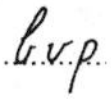 instead of the links 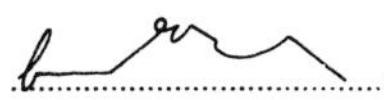 and 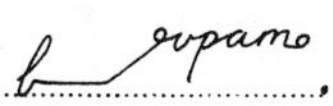.

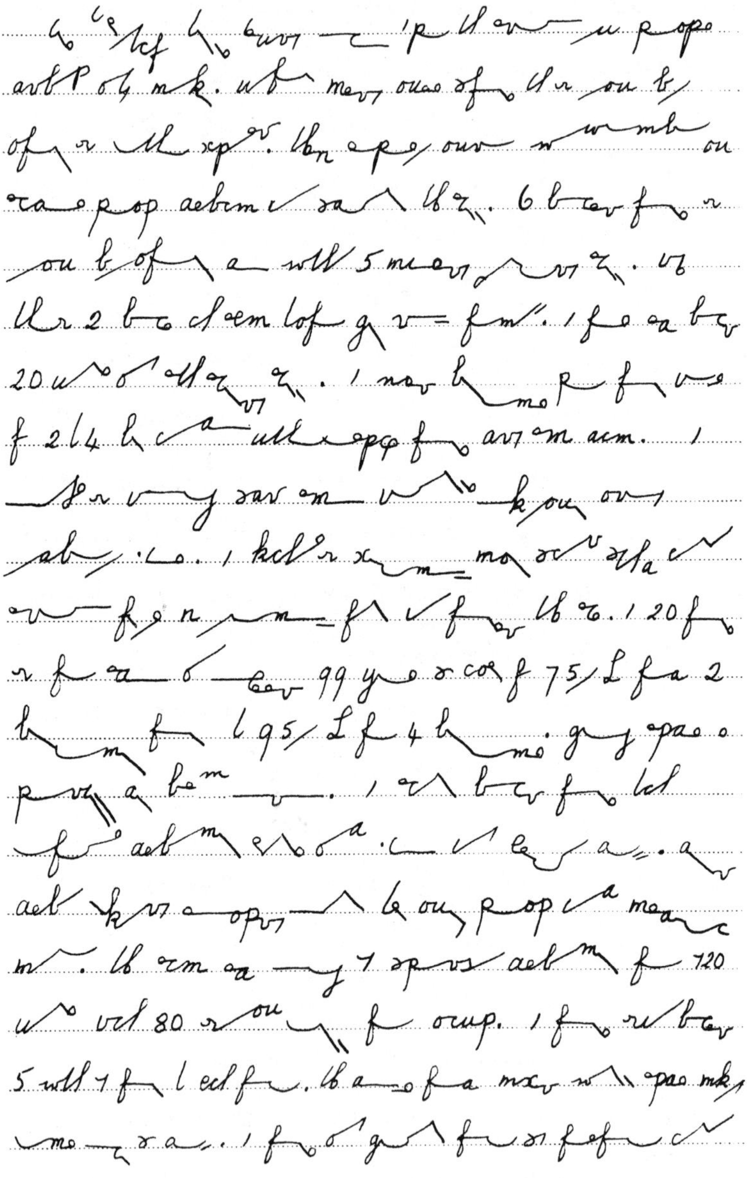

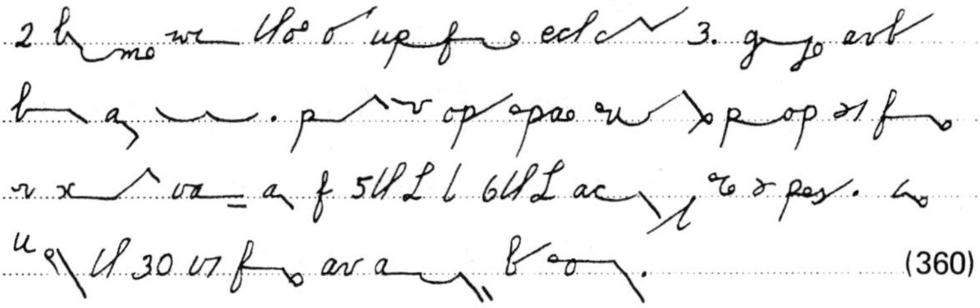

(360)

Pitman Examinations Institute

72

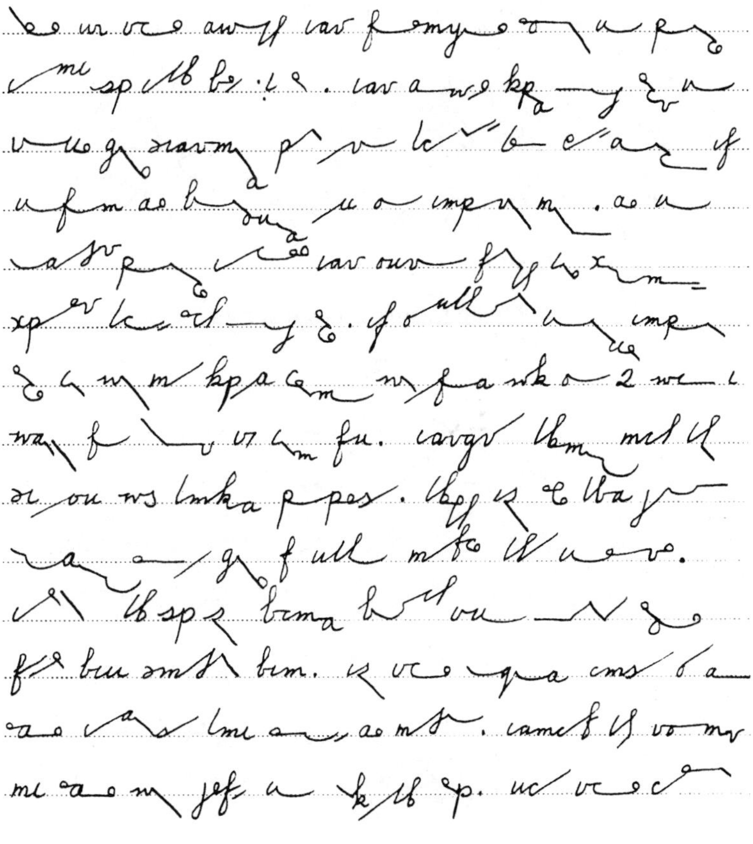

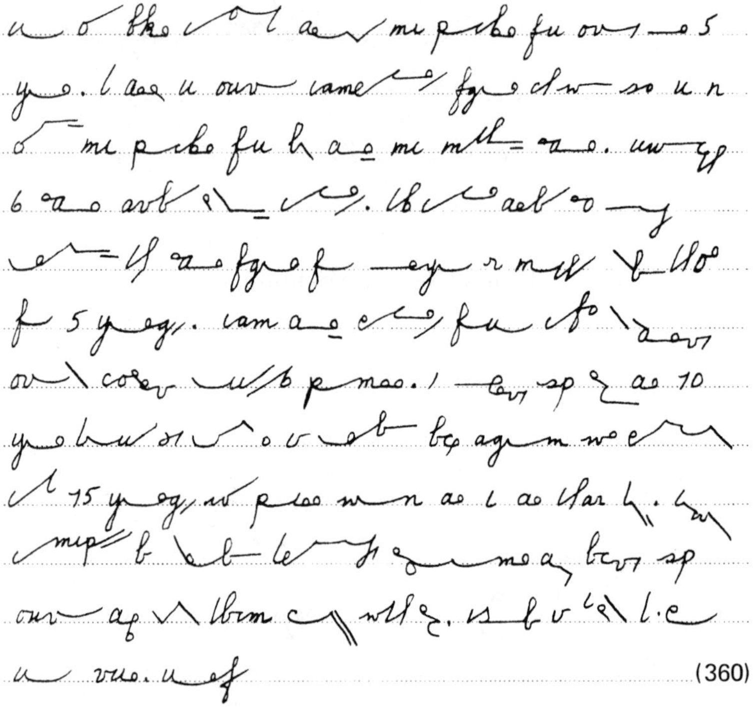

(360)

Pitman Examinations Institute

73

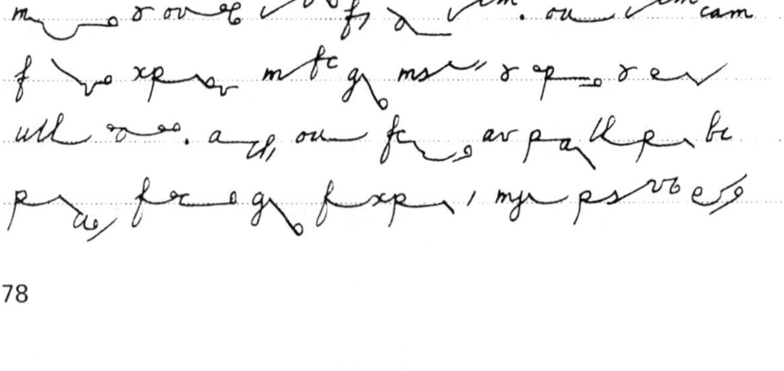

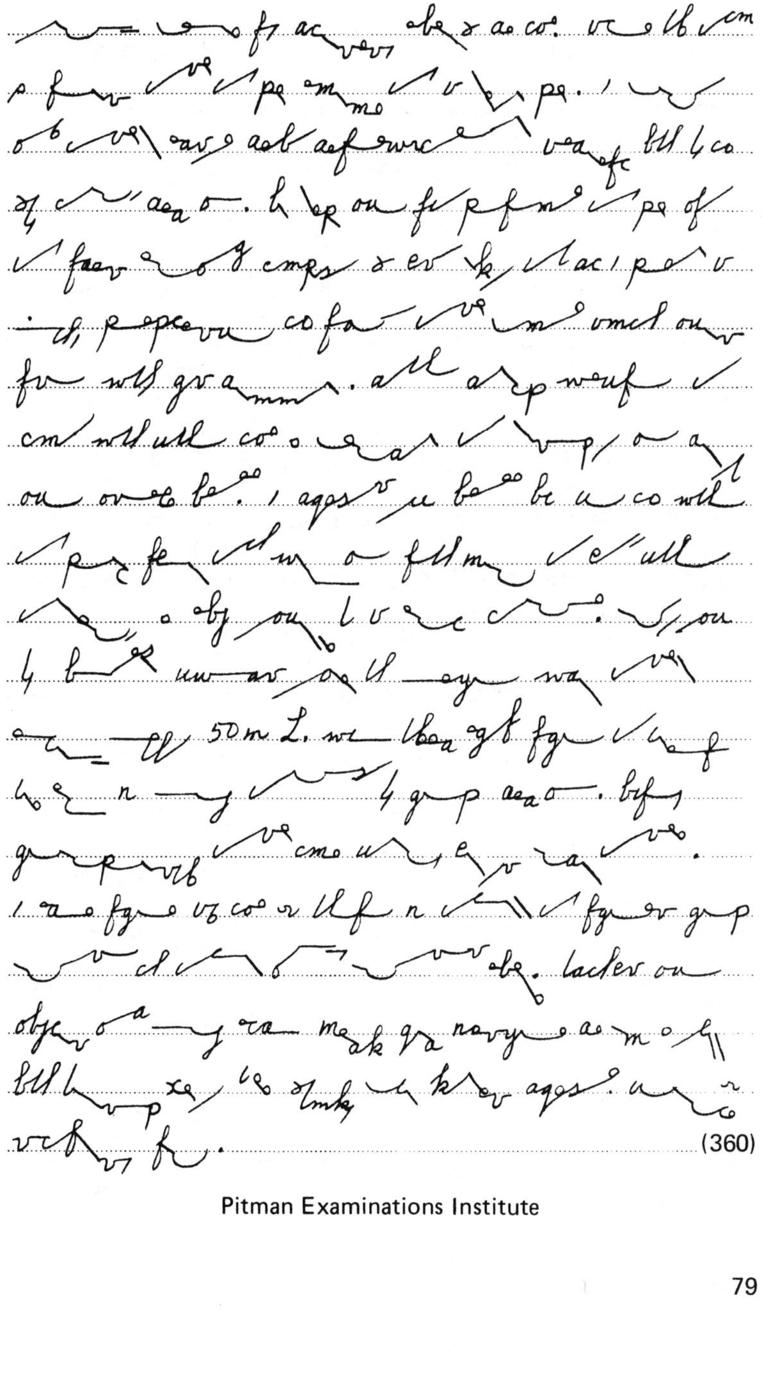

(360)

Pitman Examinations Institute

74

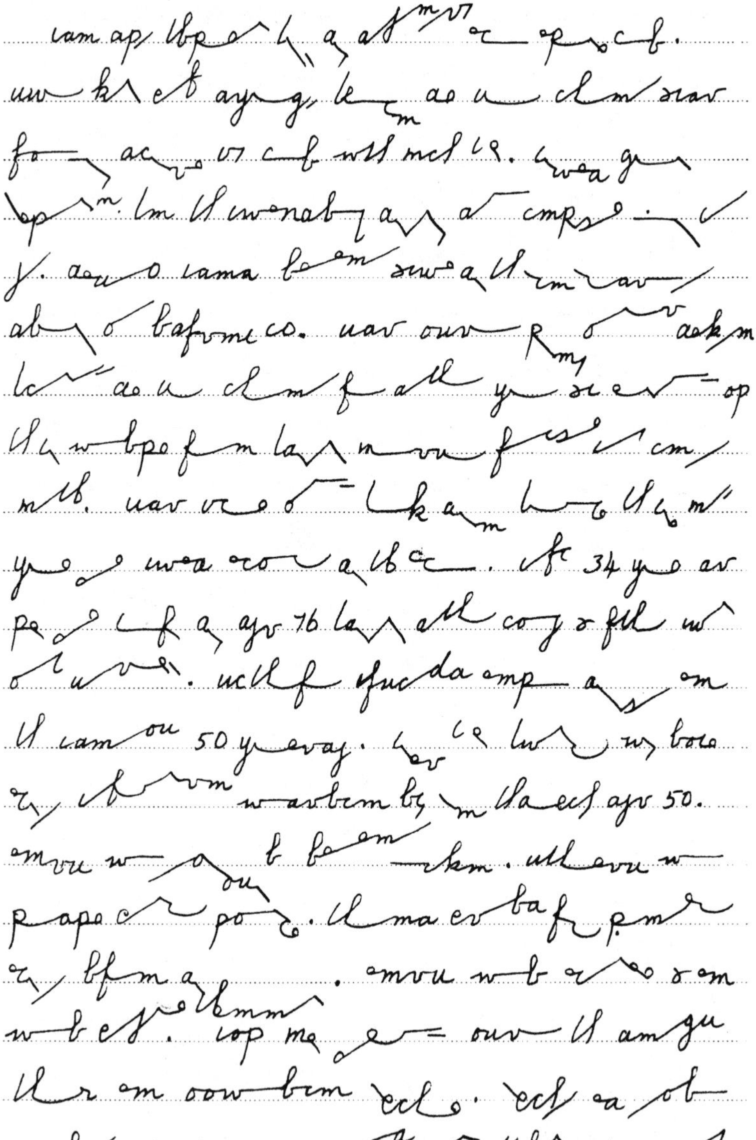

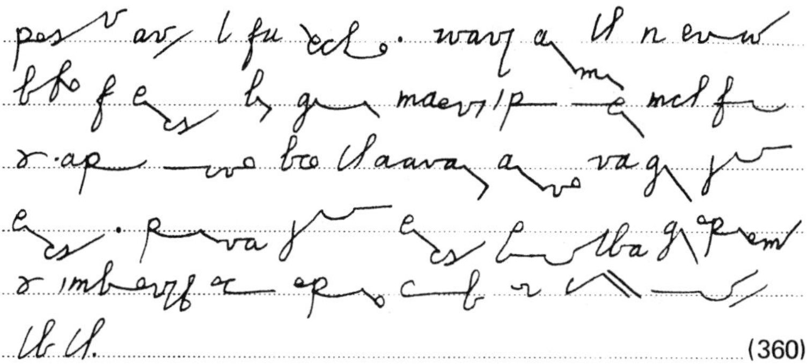

(360)

Pitman Examinations Institute

75

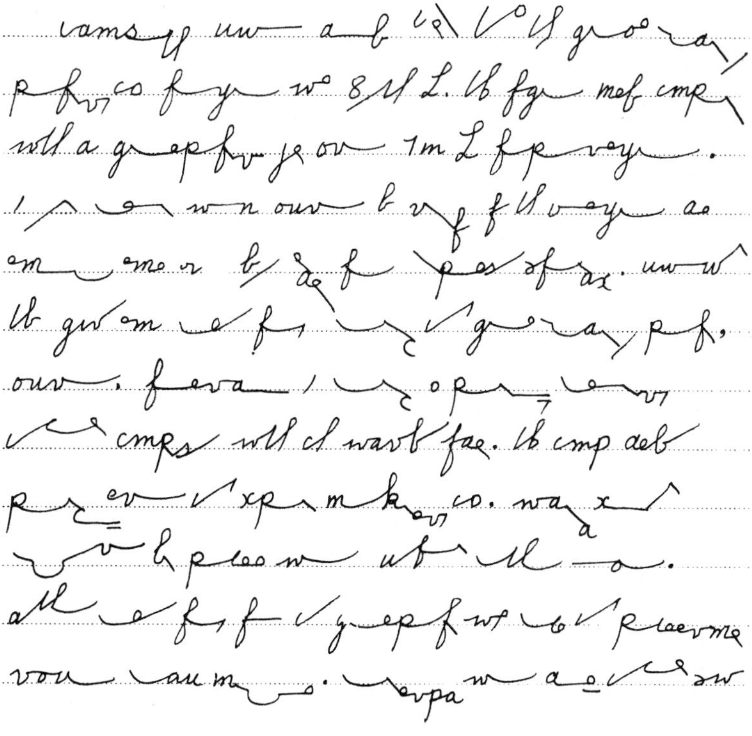

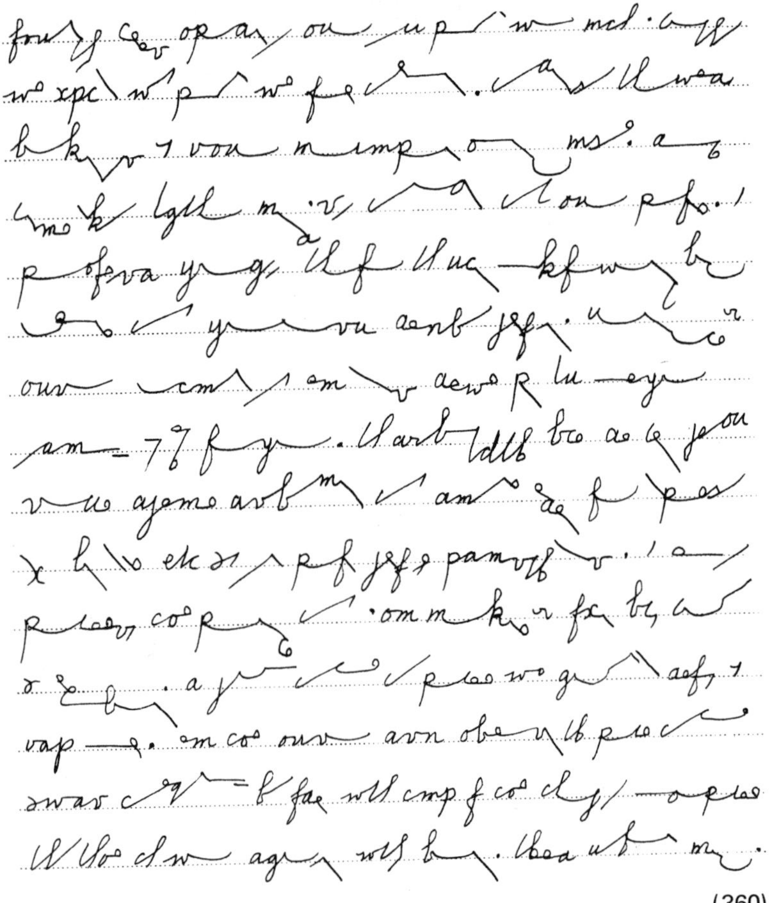

(360)

Pitman Examinations Institute

76

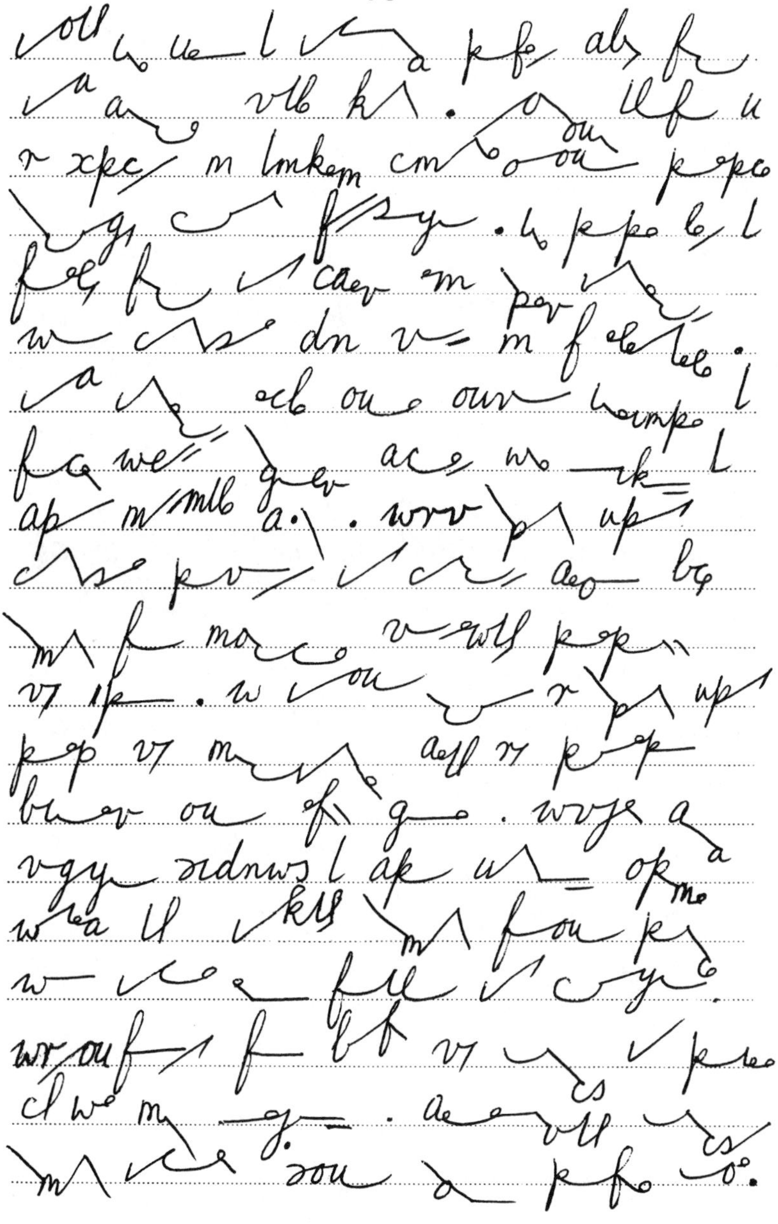

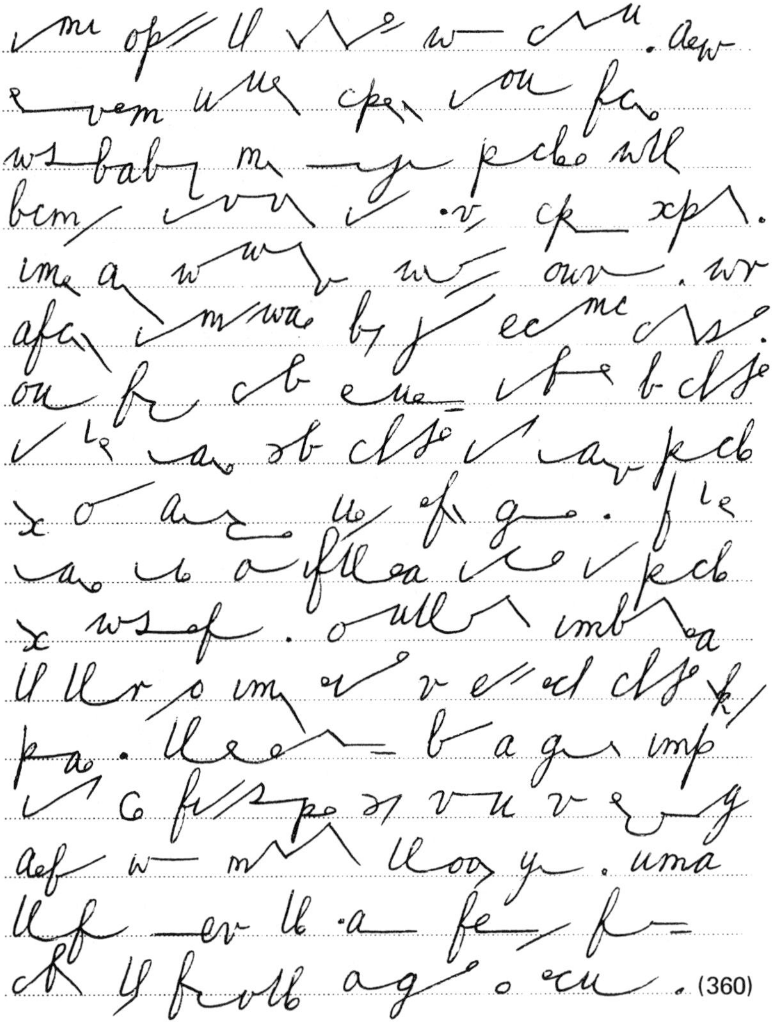

(360)

Pitman Examinations Institute

77

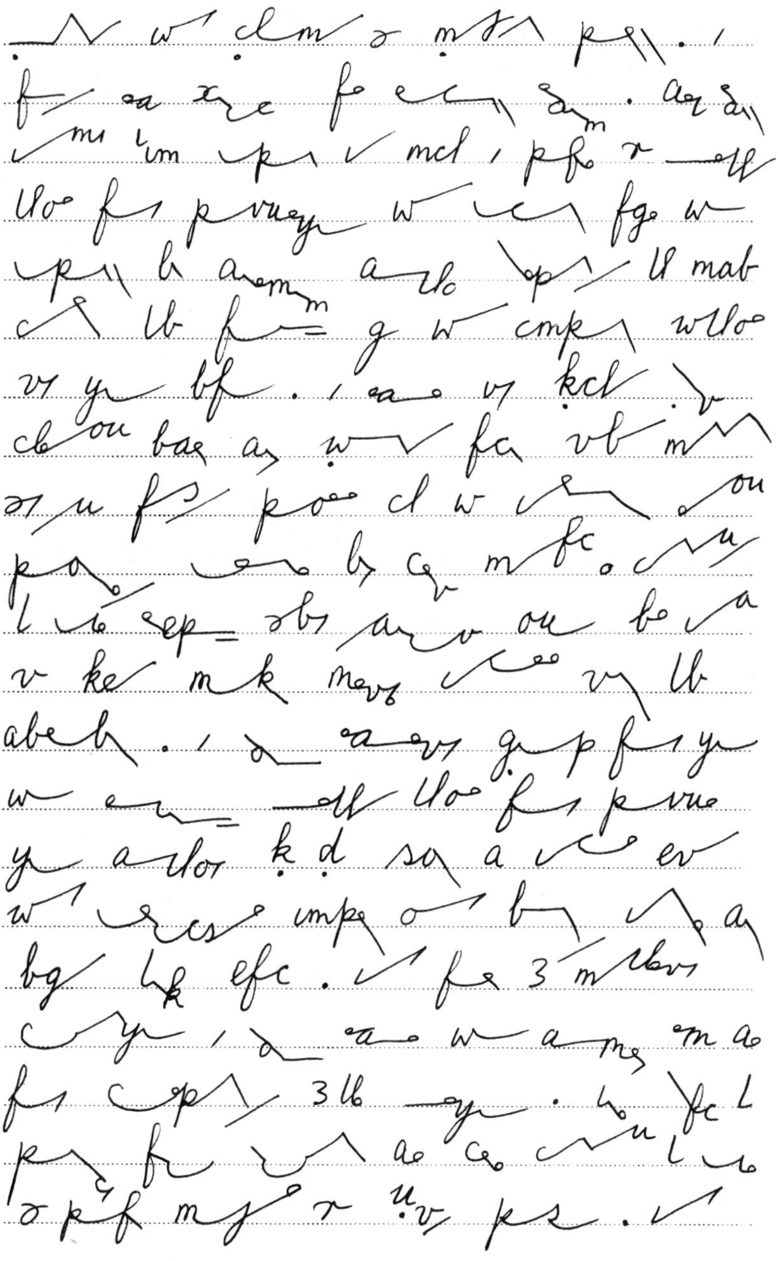

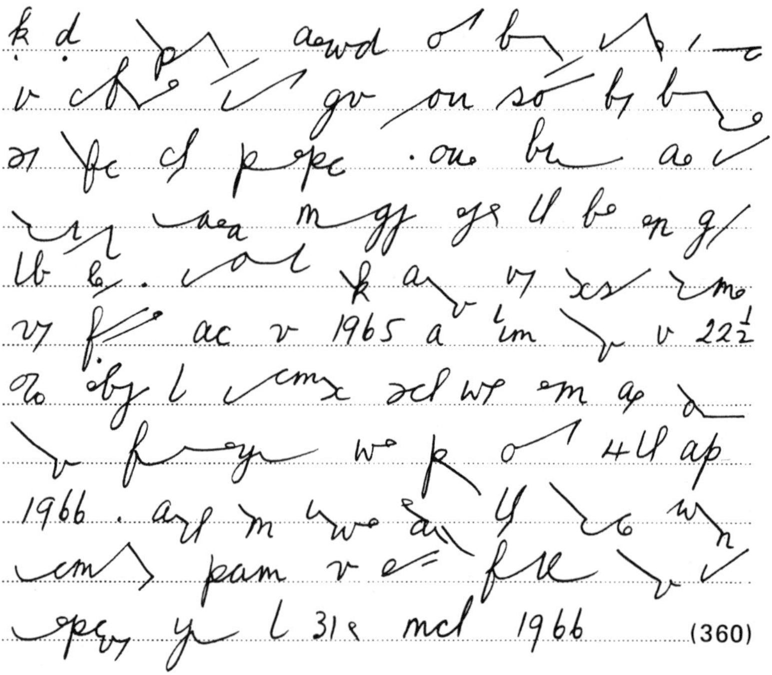

(360)

East Midland Educational Union

78

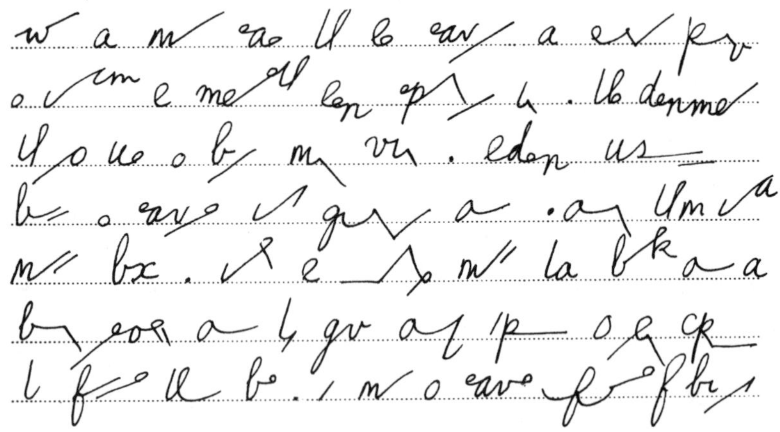

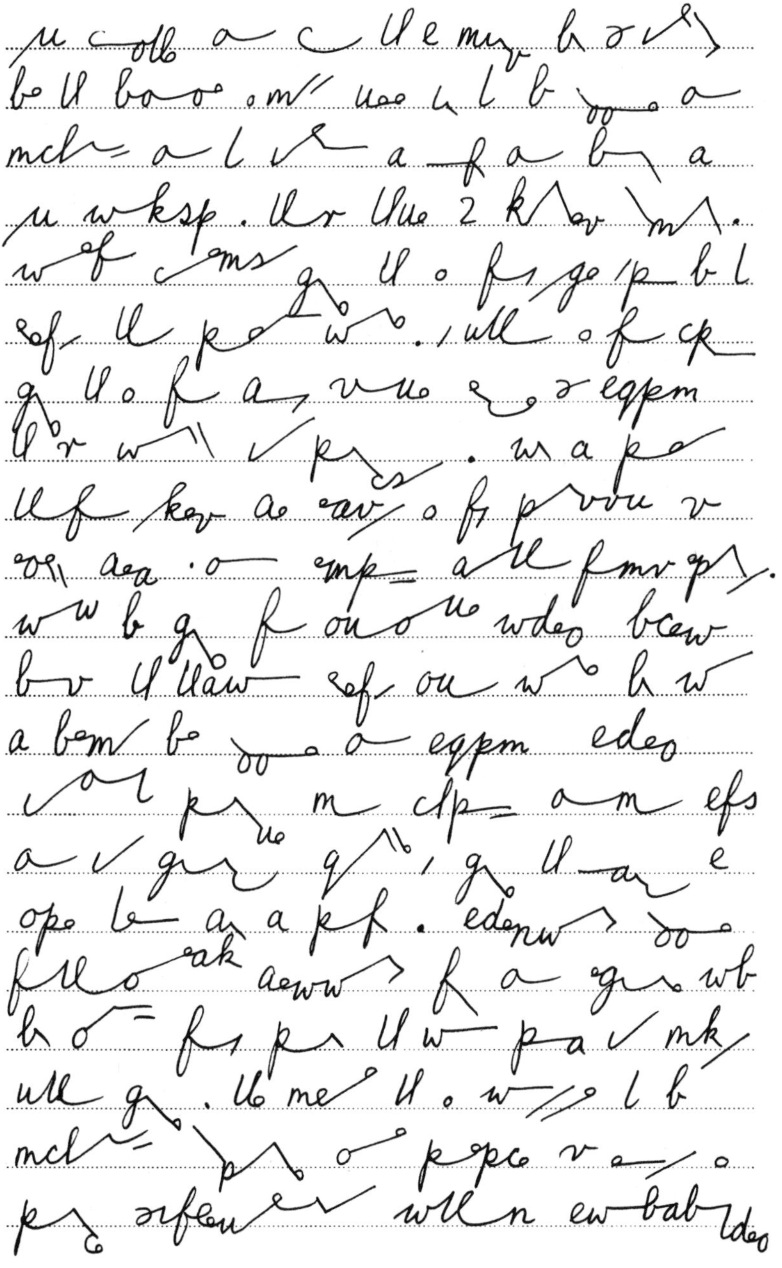

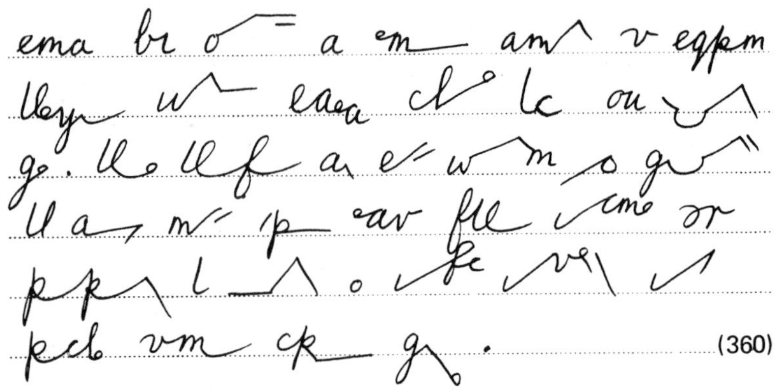

(360)

Pitman Examinations Institute

79

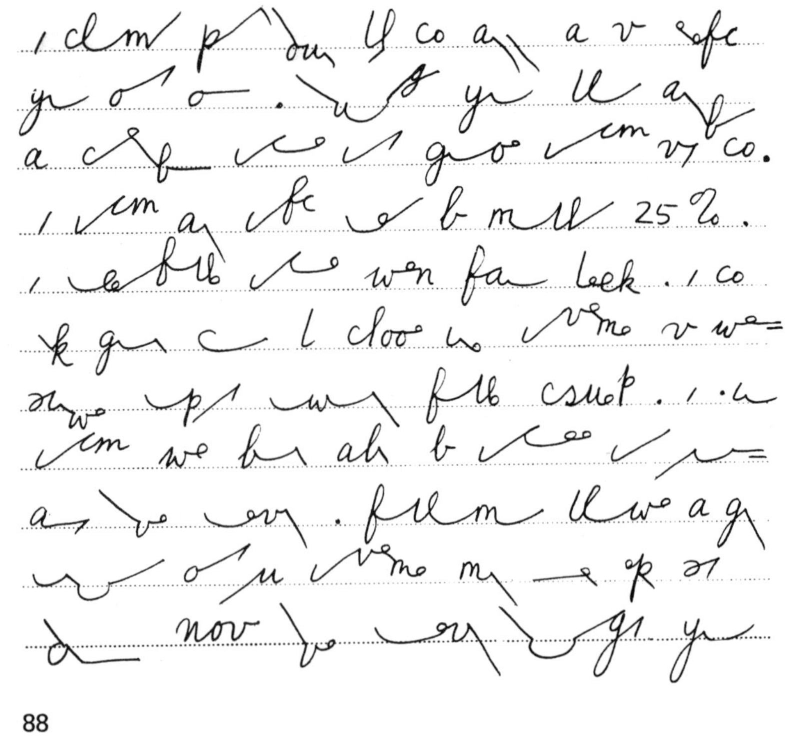

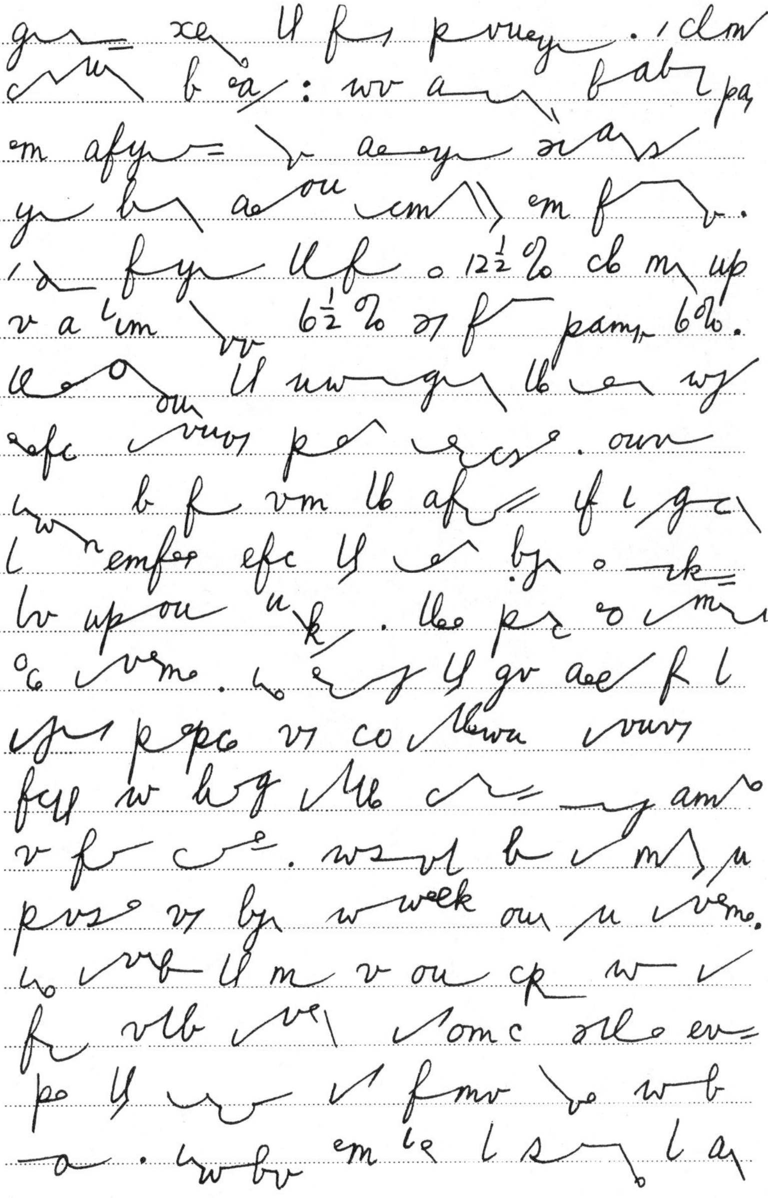

(360)

Pitman Examinations Institute

80

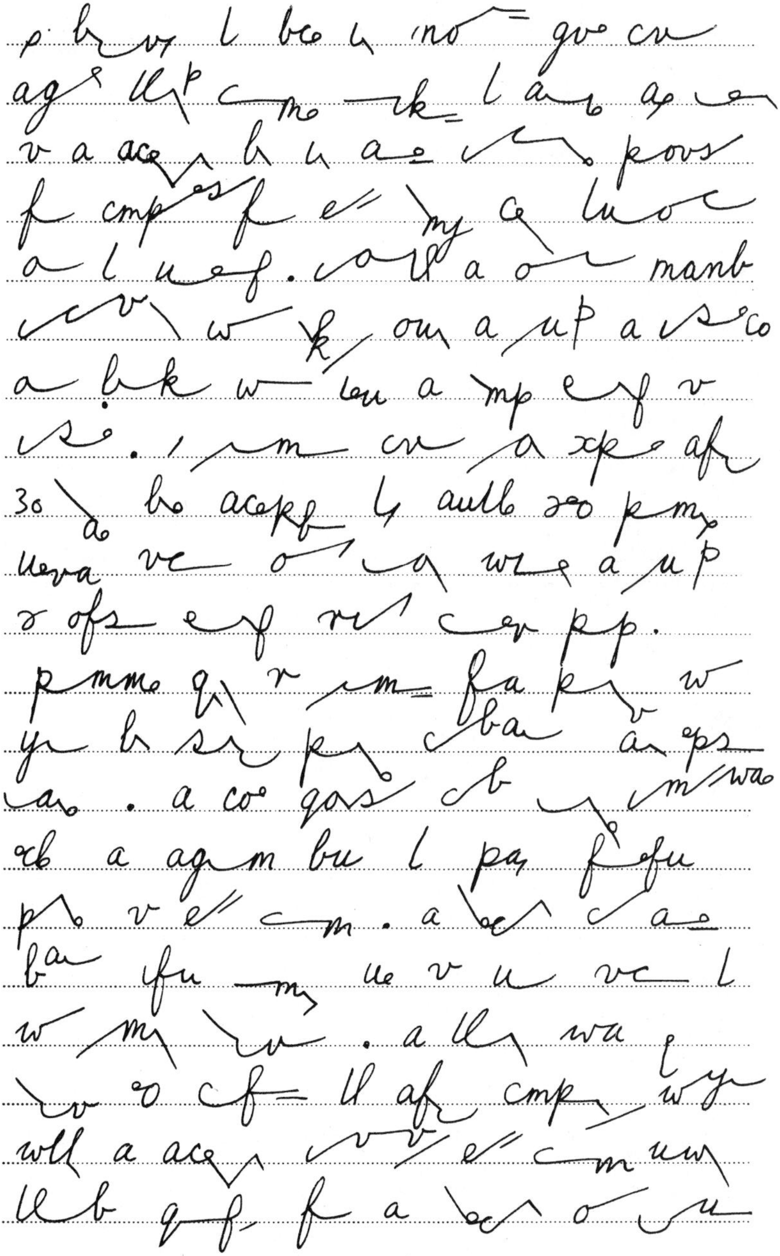

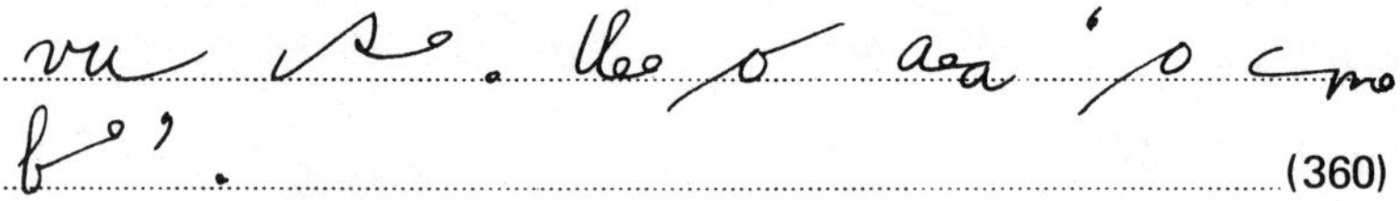

(360)

Welsh Joint Education Committee

81

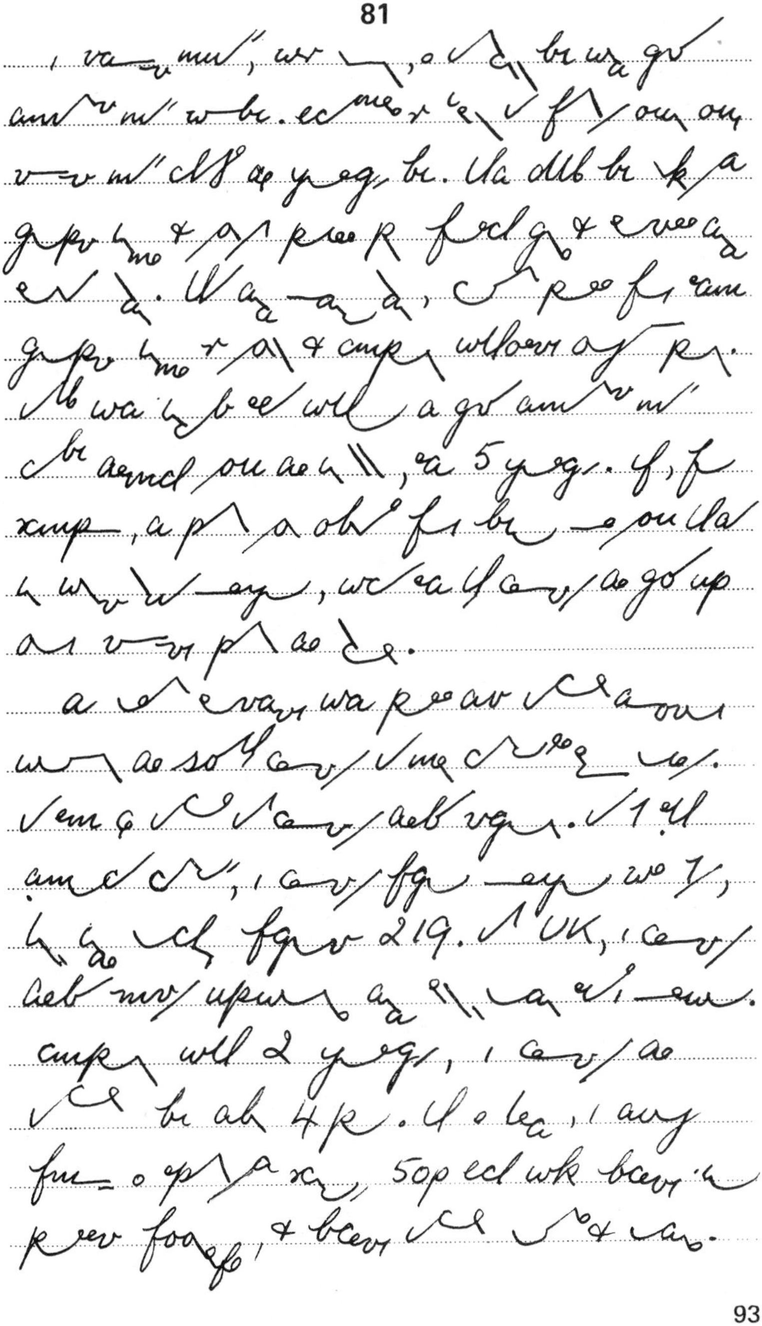

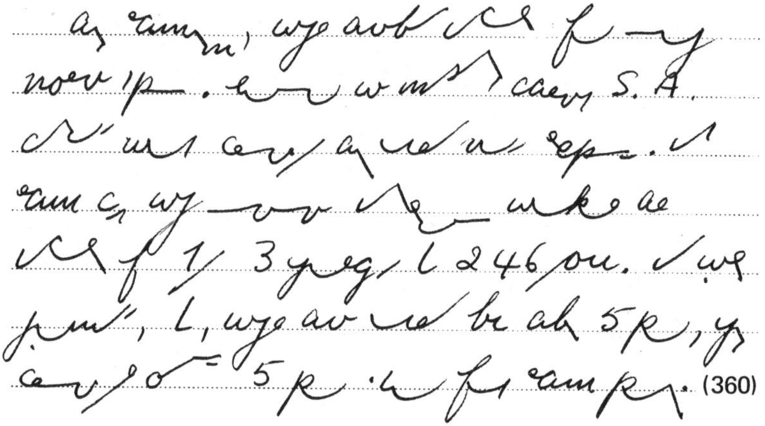

(360)

Pitman Examinations Institute

82

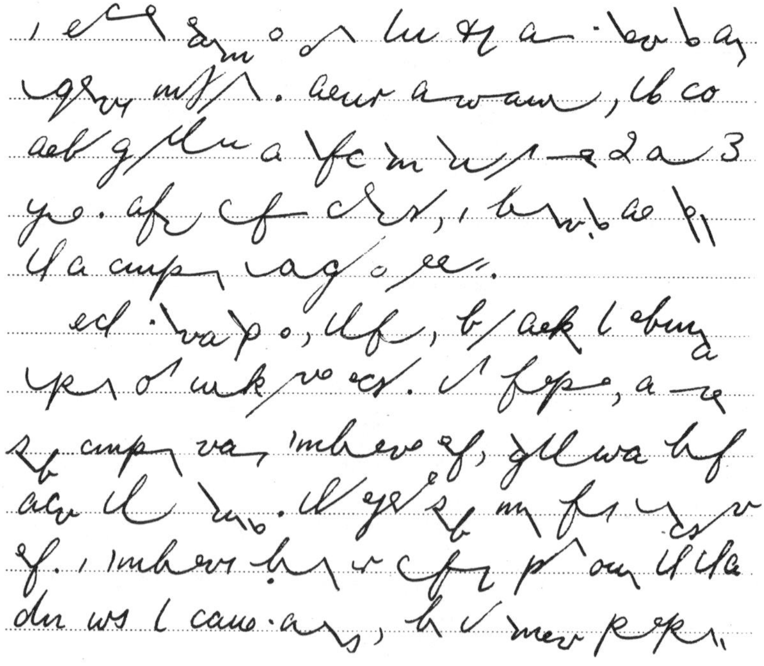

(360)

Pitman Examinations Institute

83

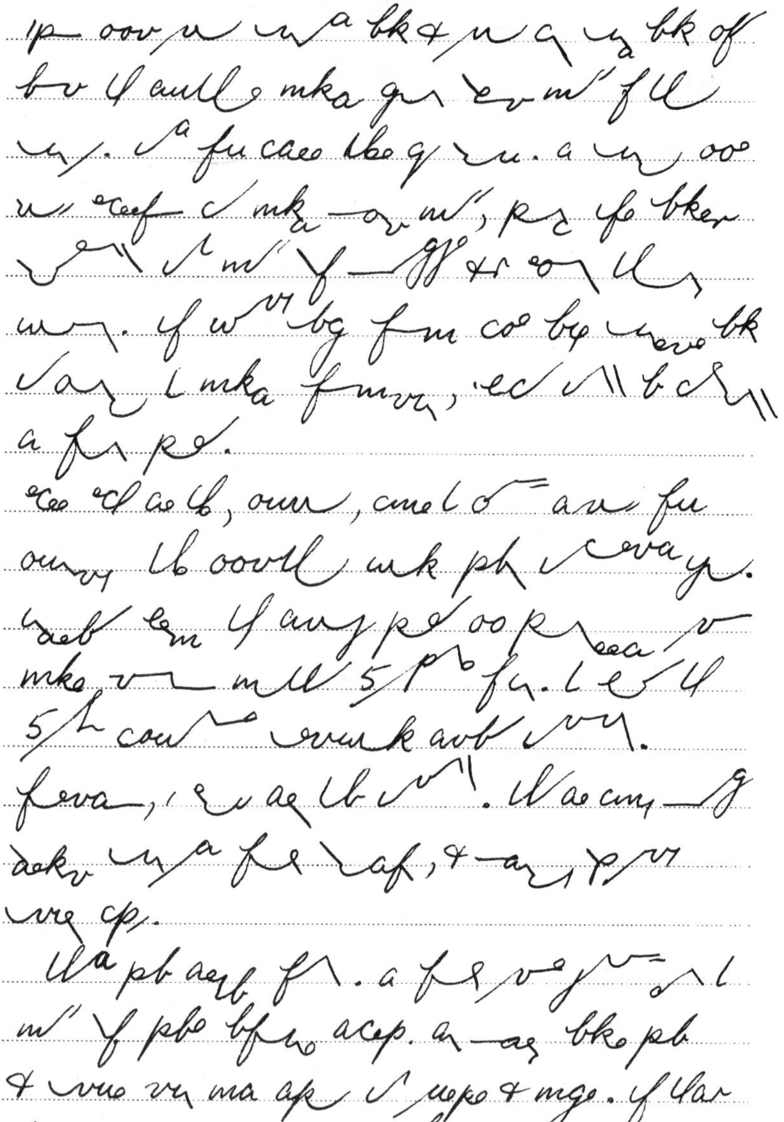

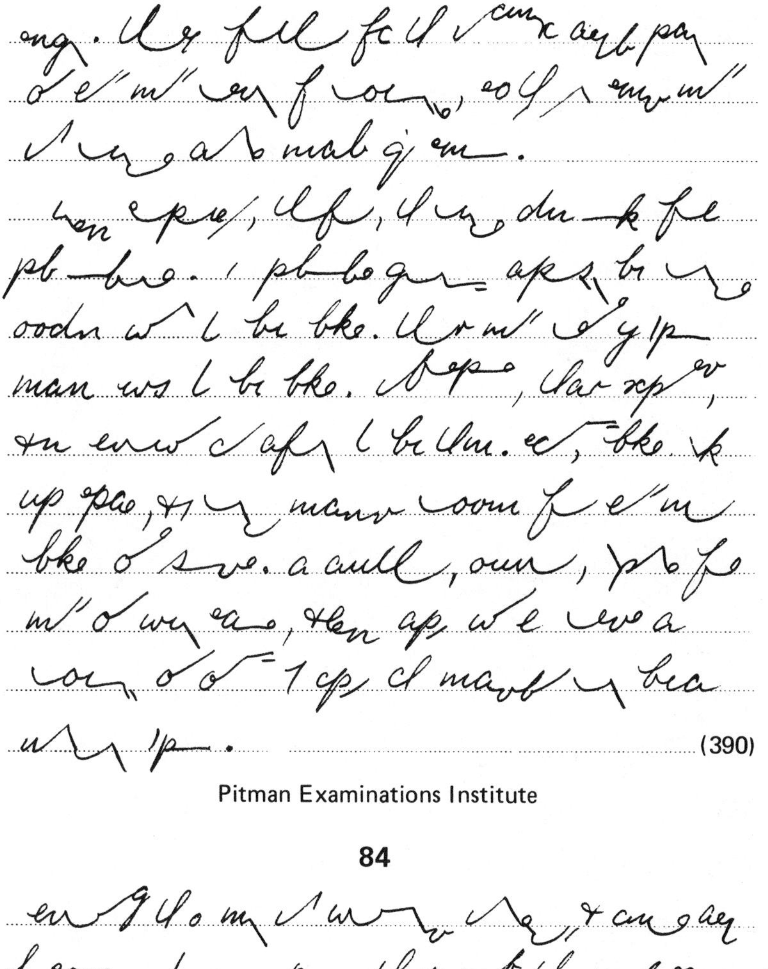

(390)

Pitman Examinations Institute

84

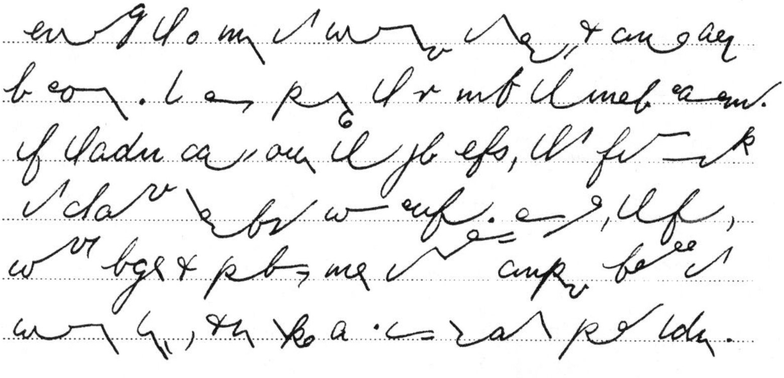

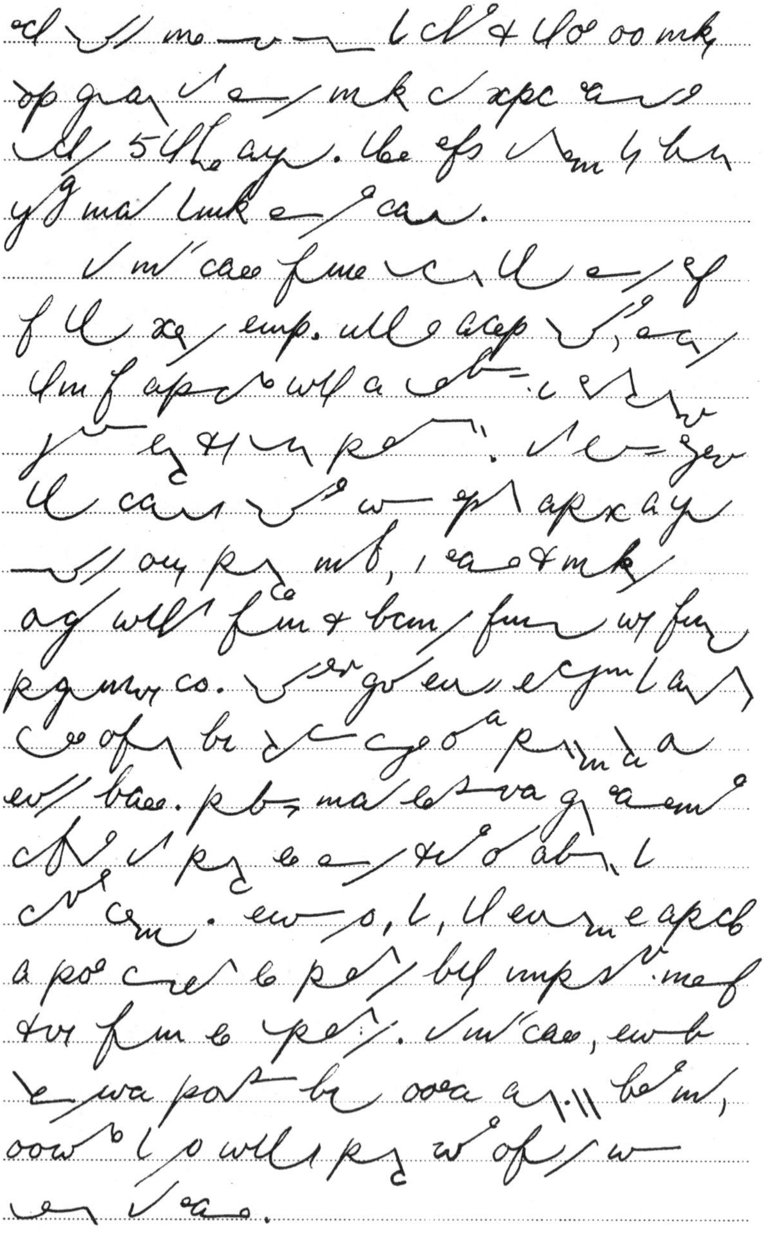

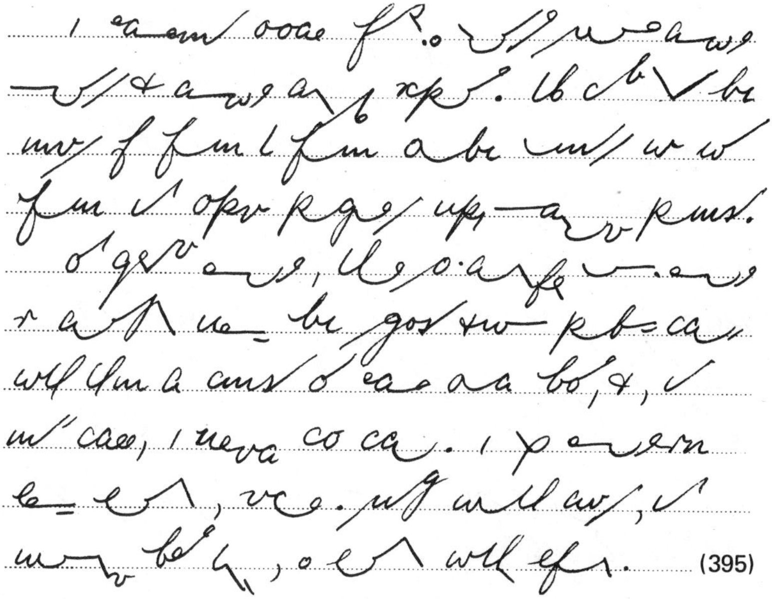

(395)

Union of Lancashire and Cheshire Institutes

85

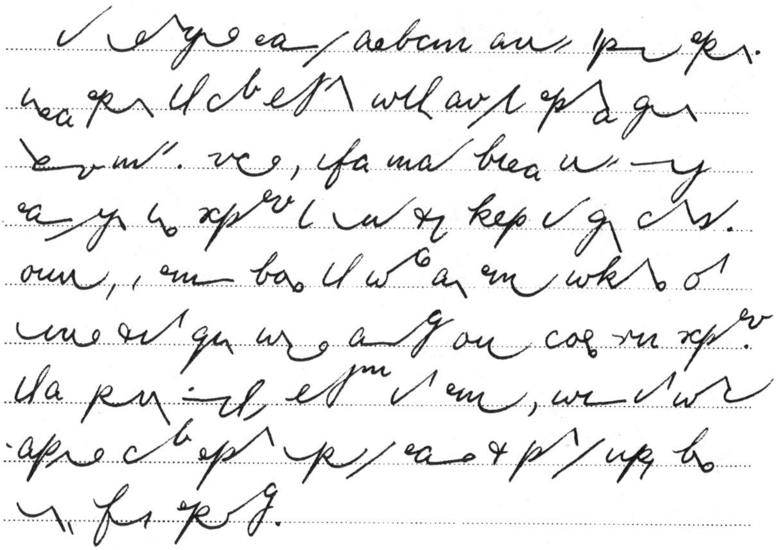

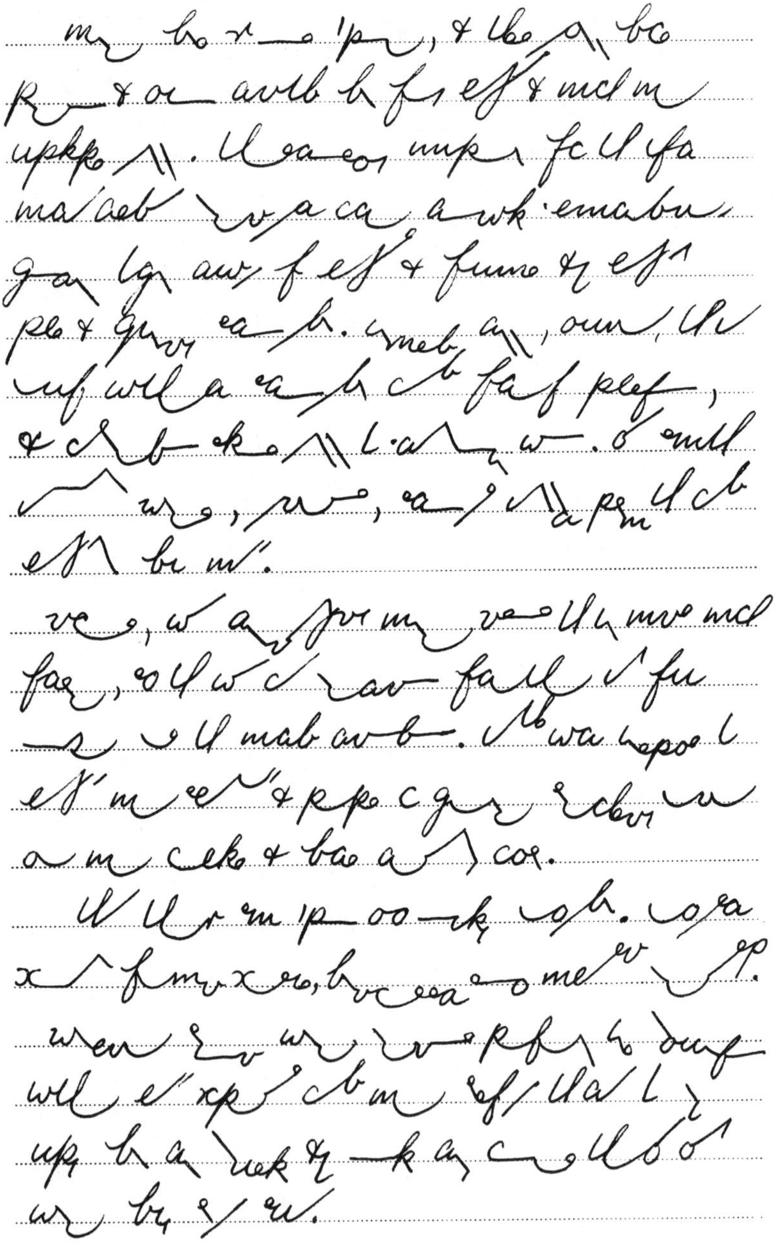

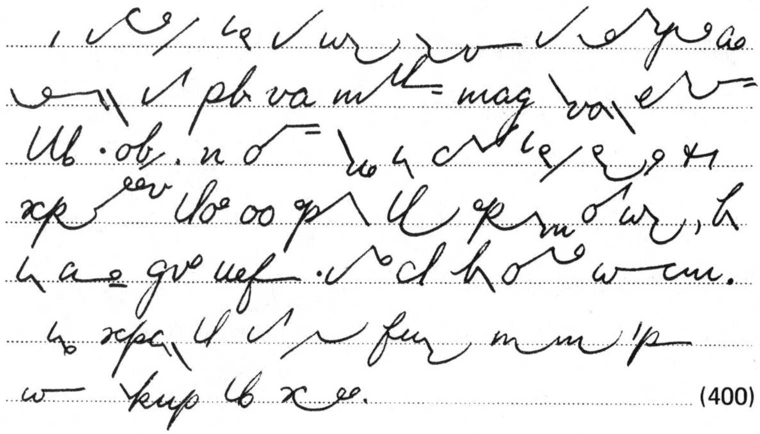

(400)

Pitman Examinations Institute

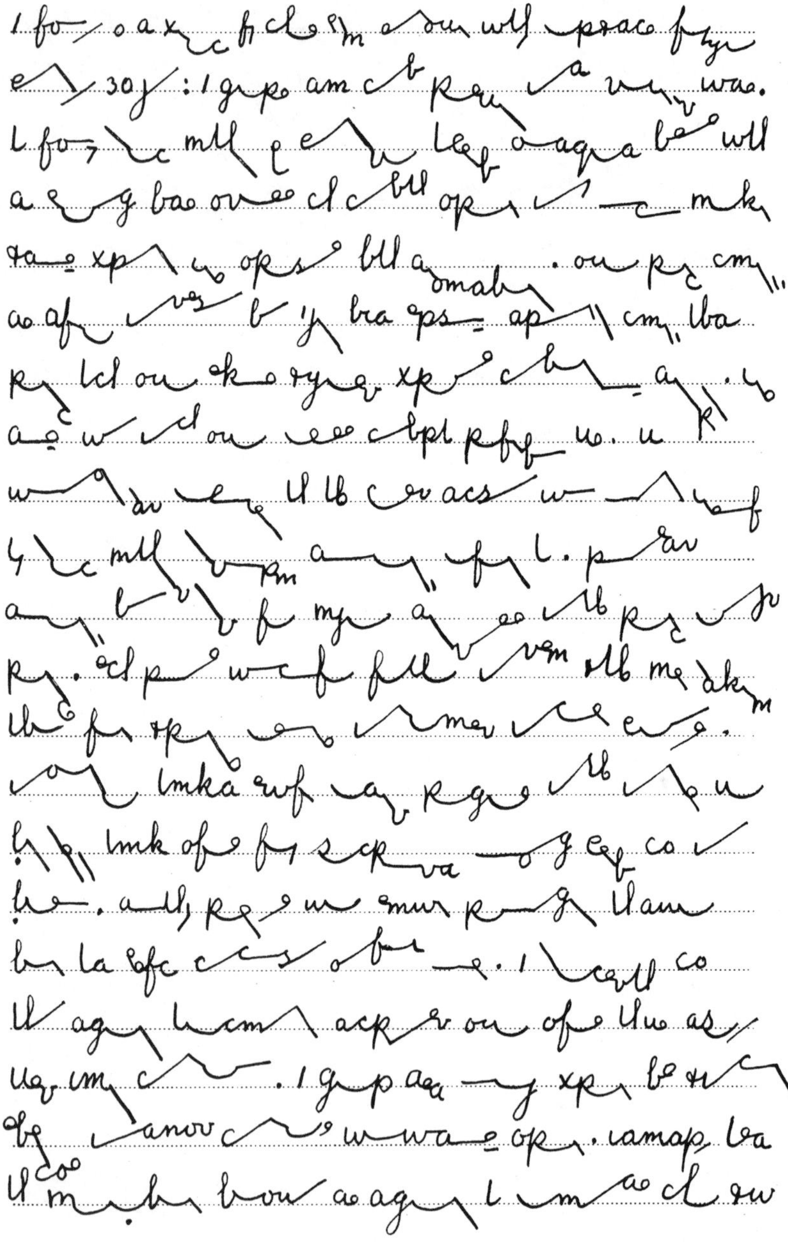

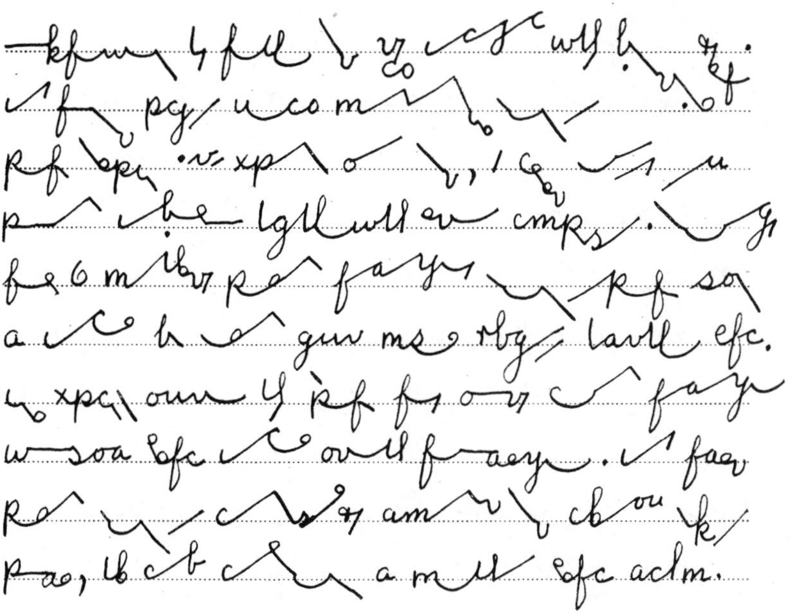

(400)

Pitman Examinations Institute

87

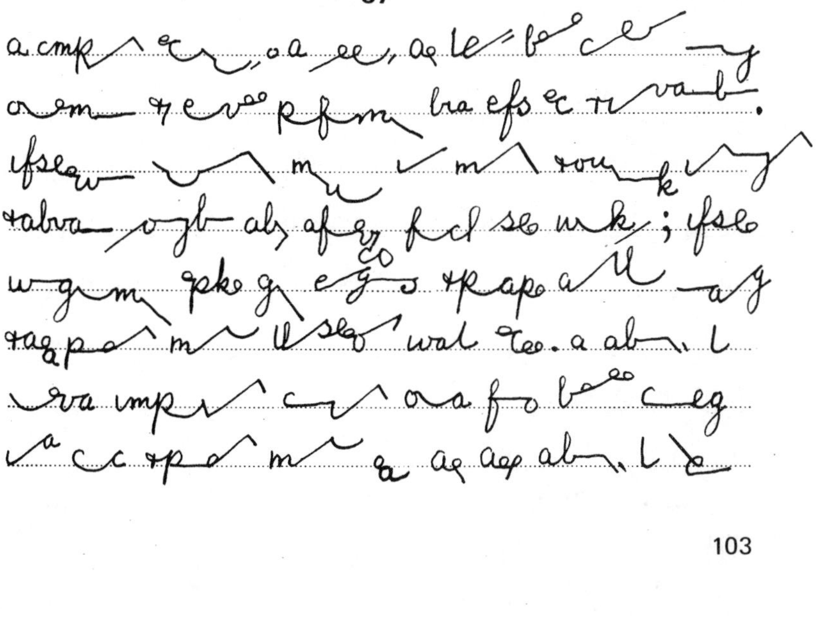

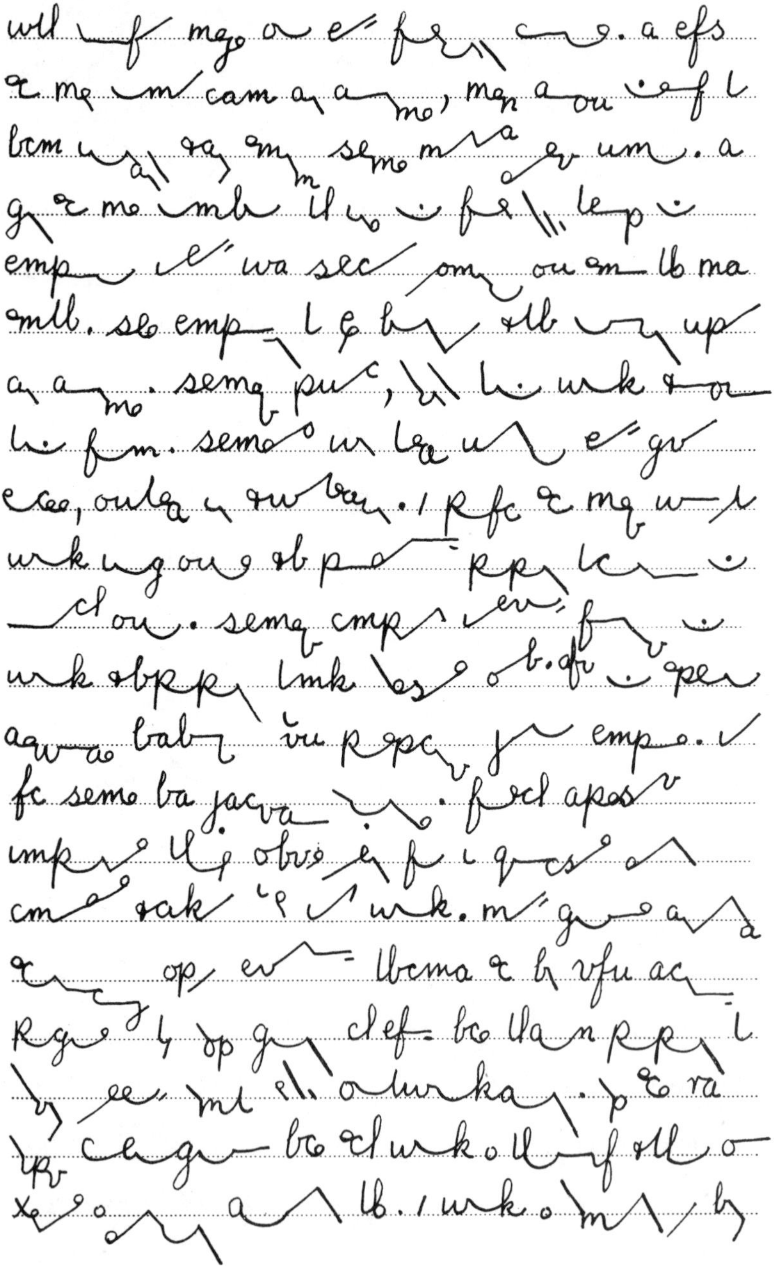

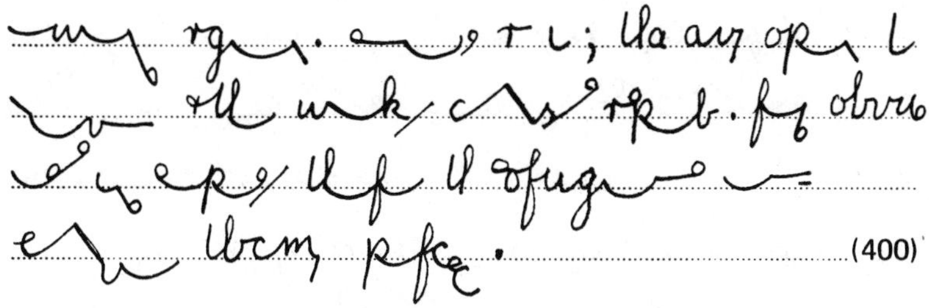

(400)

Welsh Joint Education Committee

88

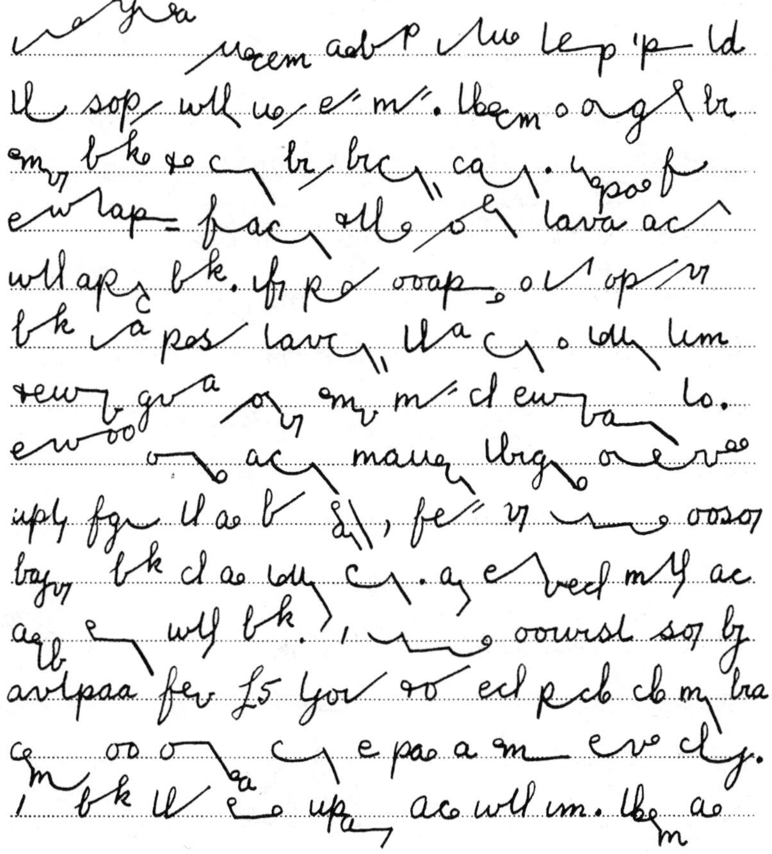

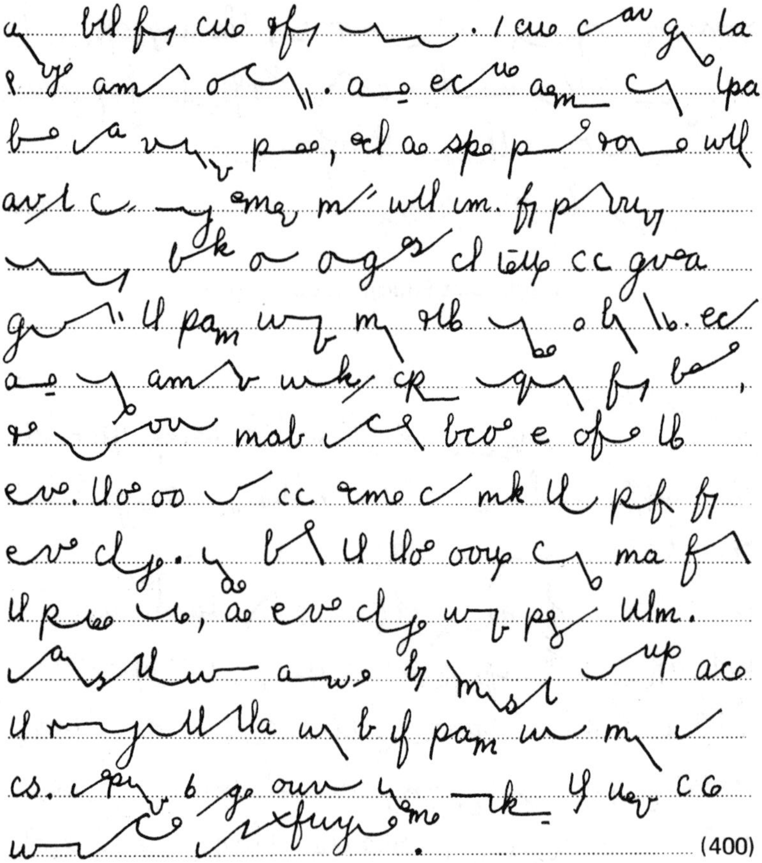

(400)

London Chamber of Commerce

89

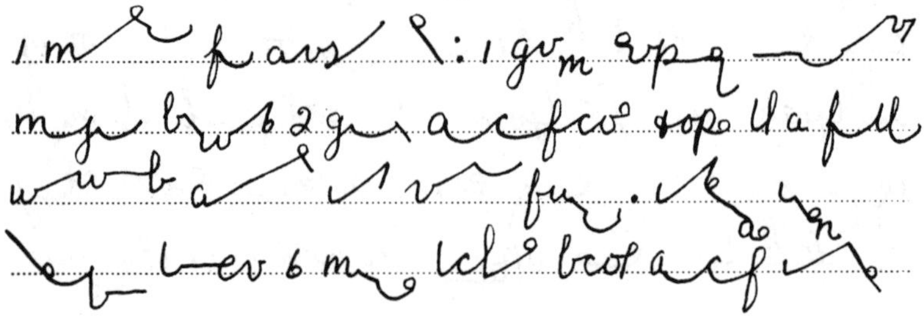

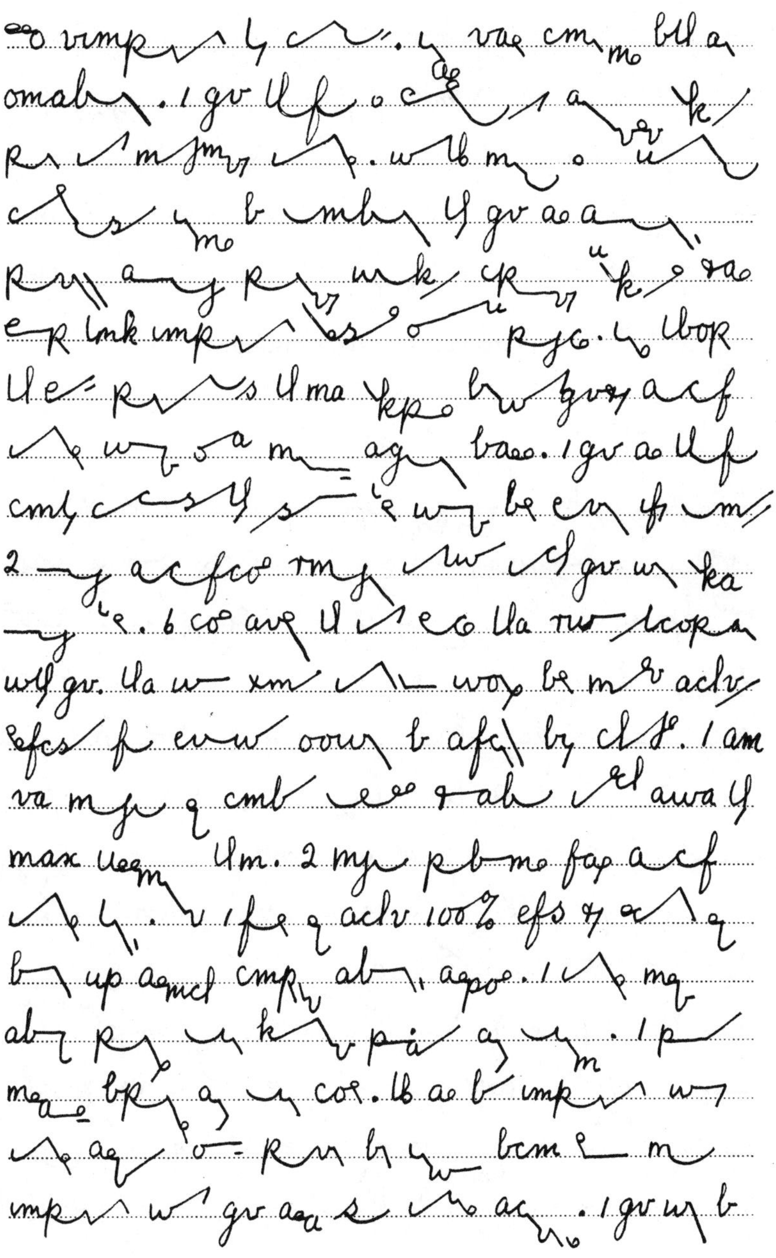

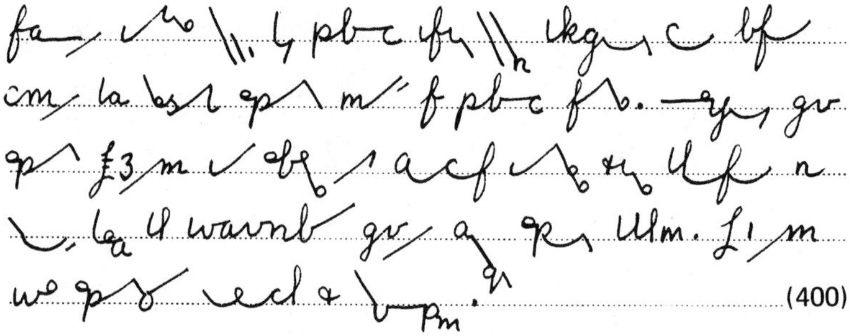

(400)

Pitman Examinations Institute

90

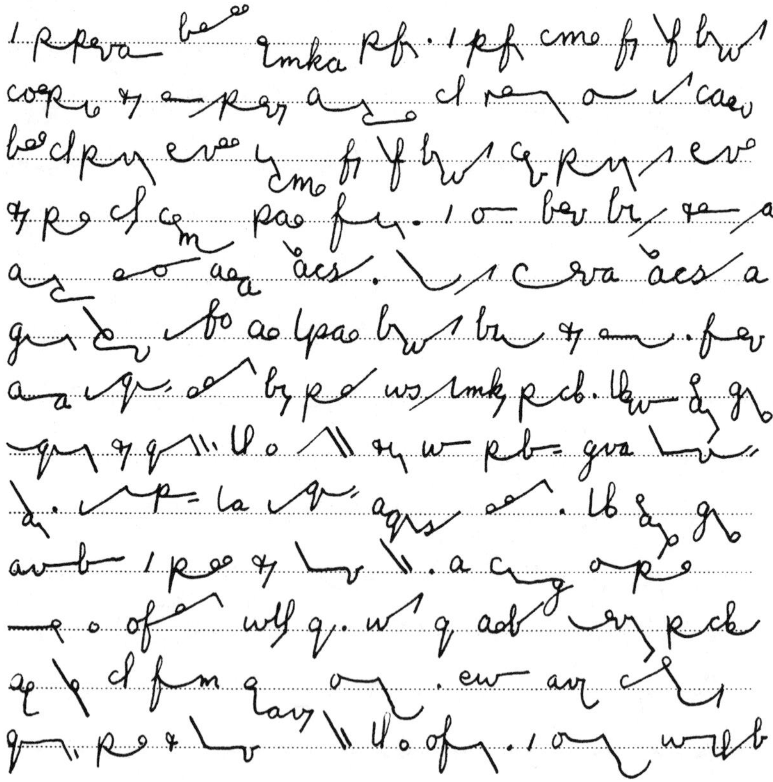

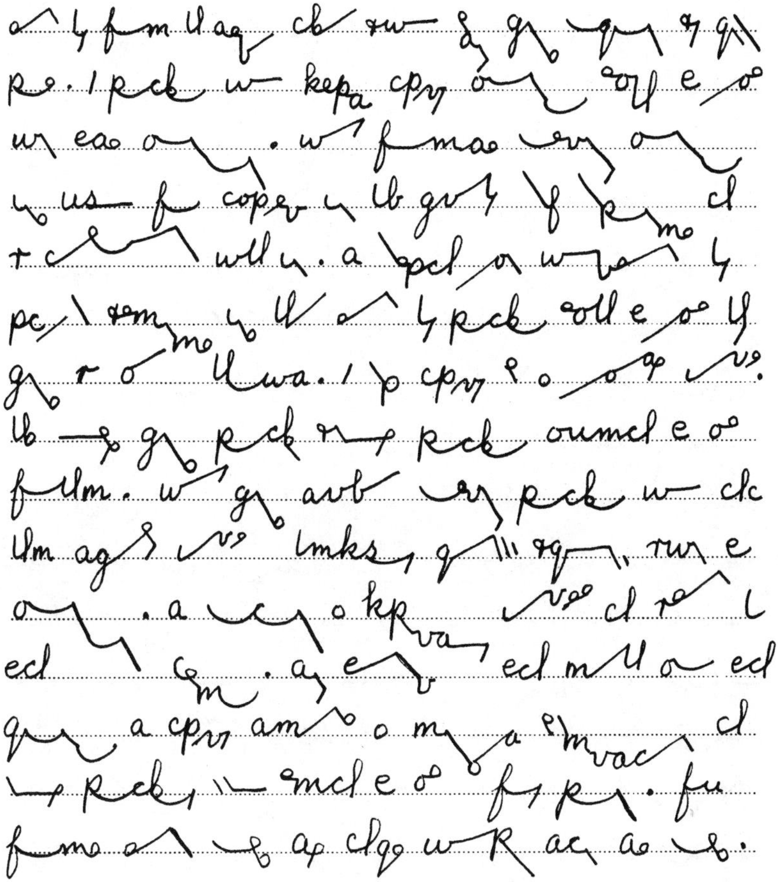

(400)

London Chamber of Commerce

91

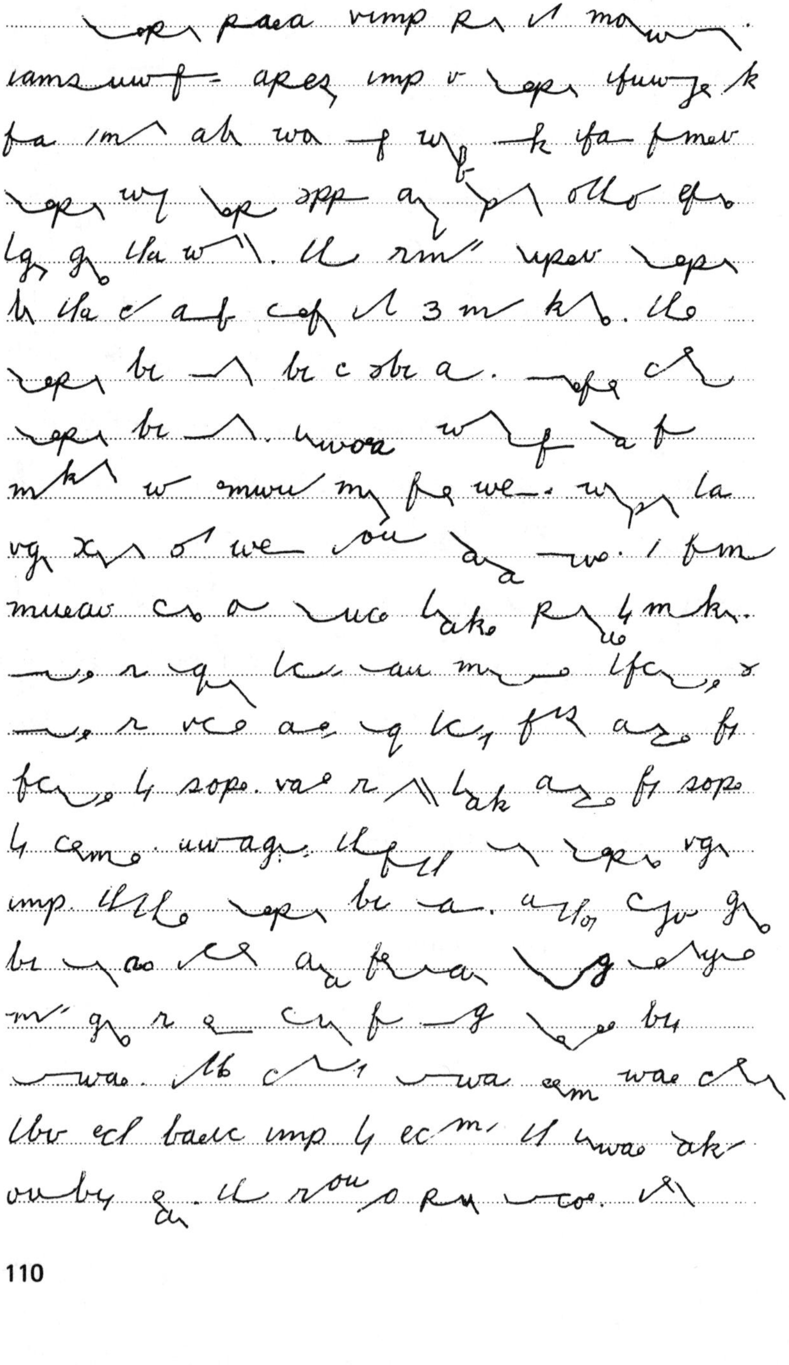

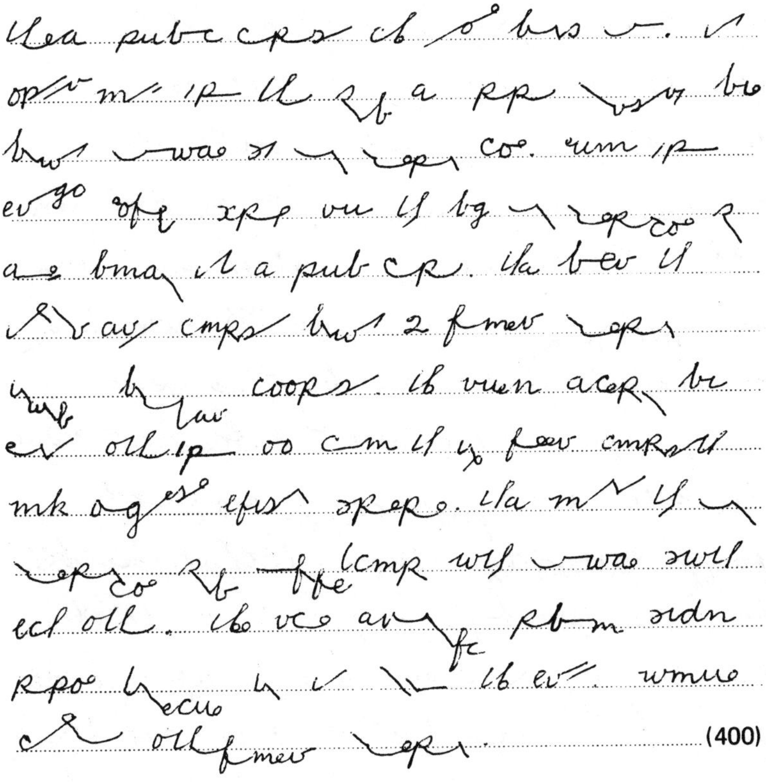

(400)

Pitman Examinations Institute

92

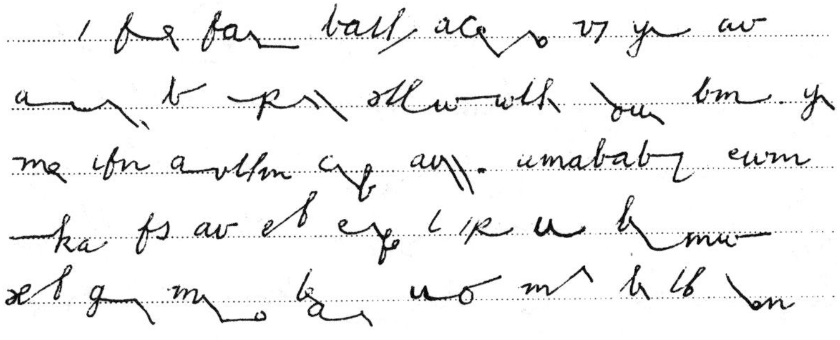

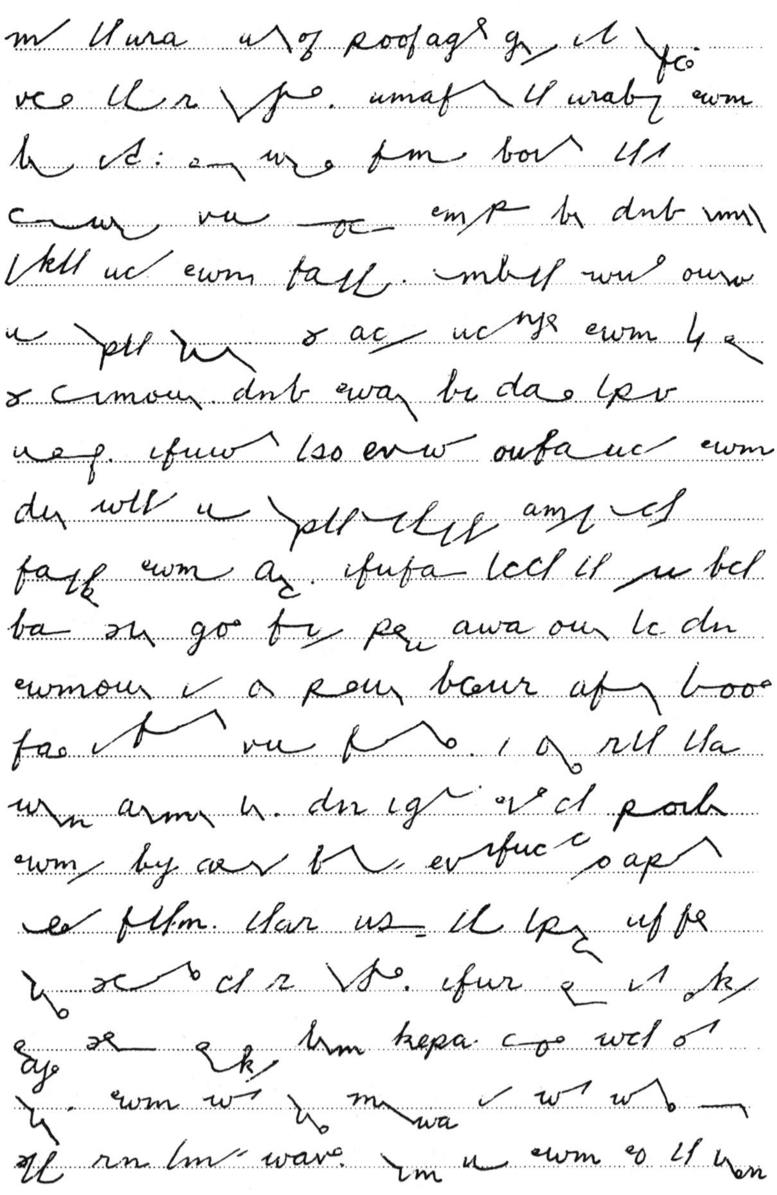

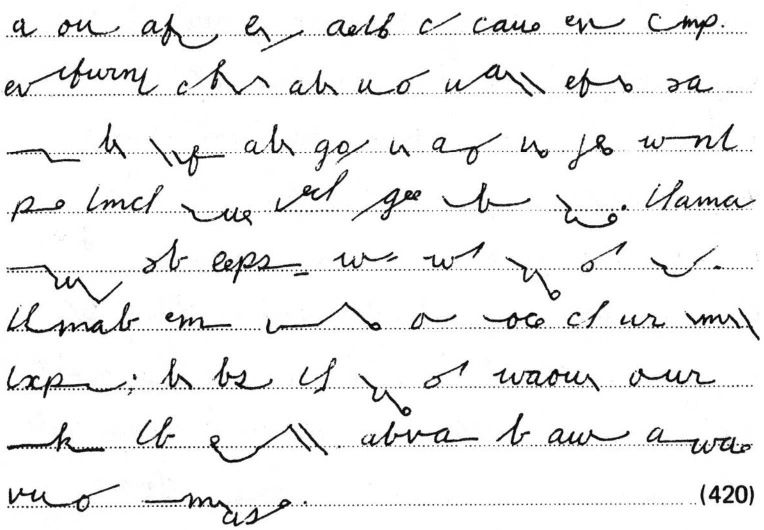

(420)

Royal Society of Arts

93

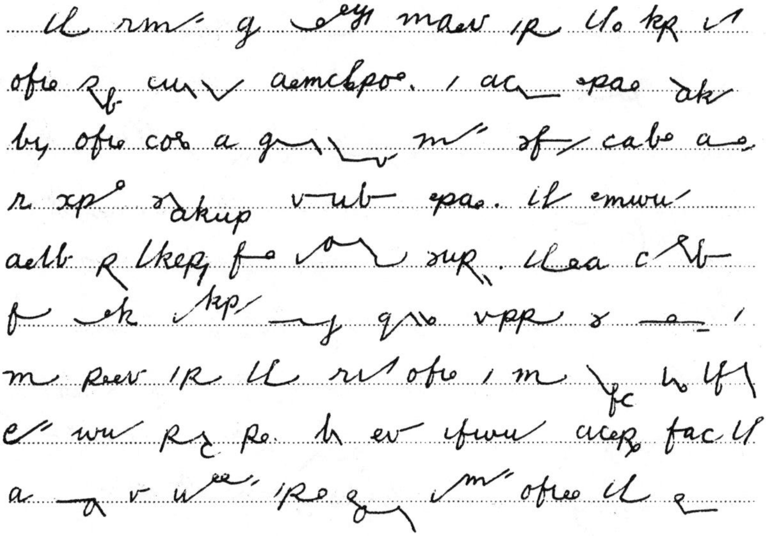

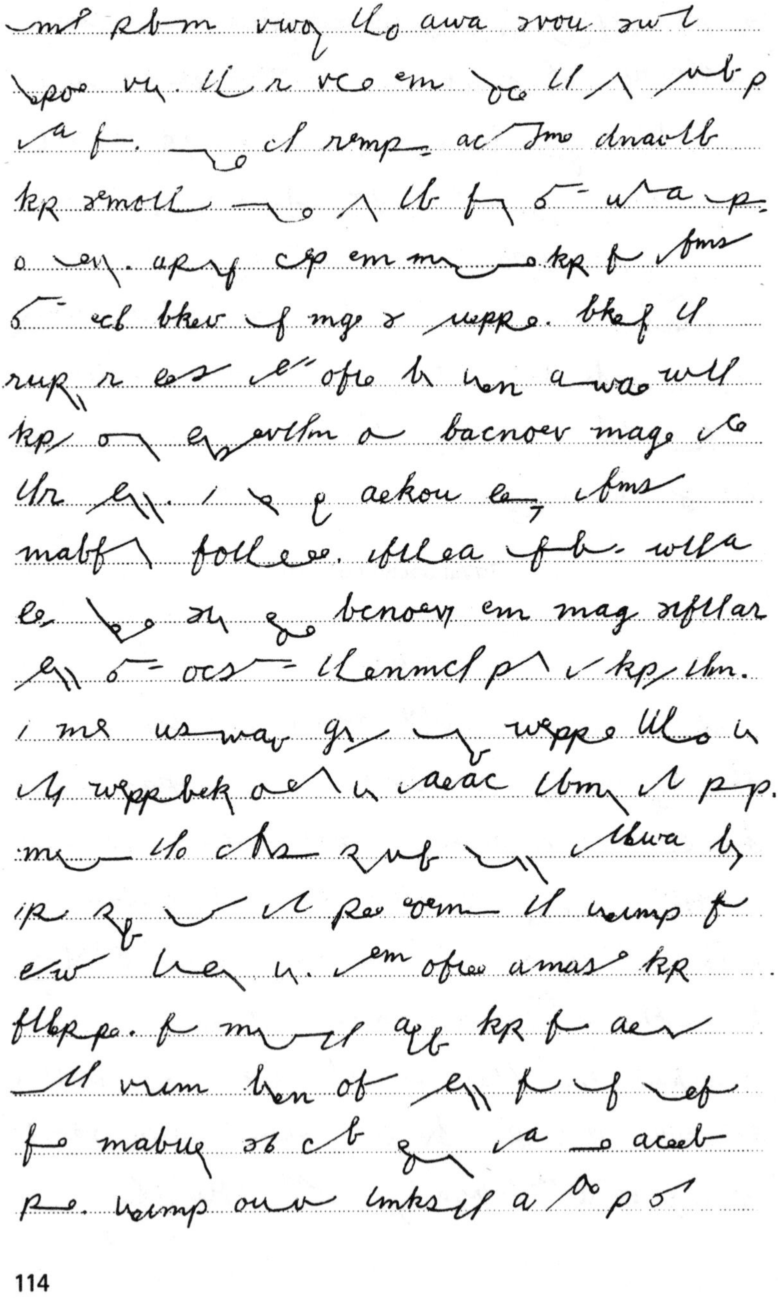

(450)

London Chamber of Commerce

94

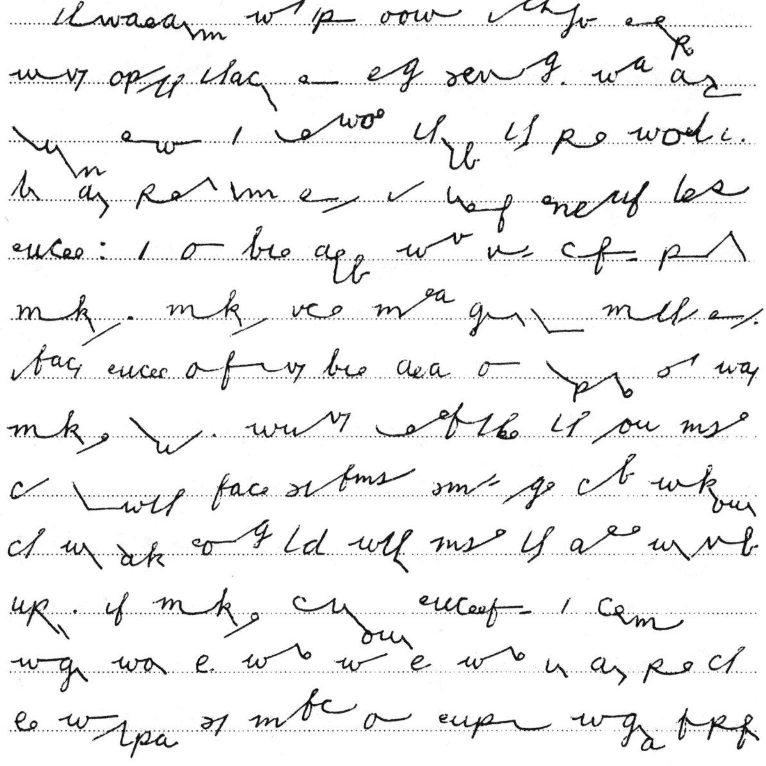

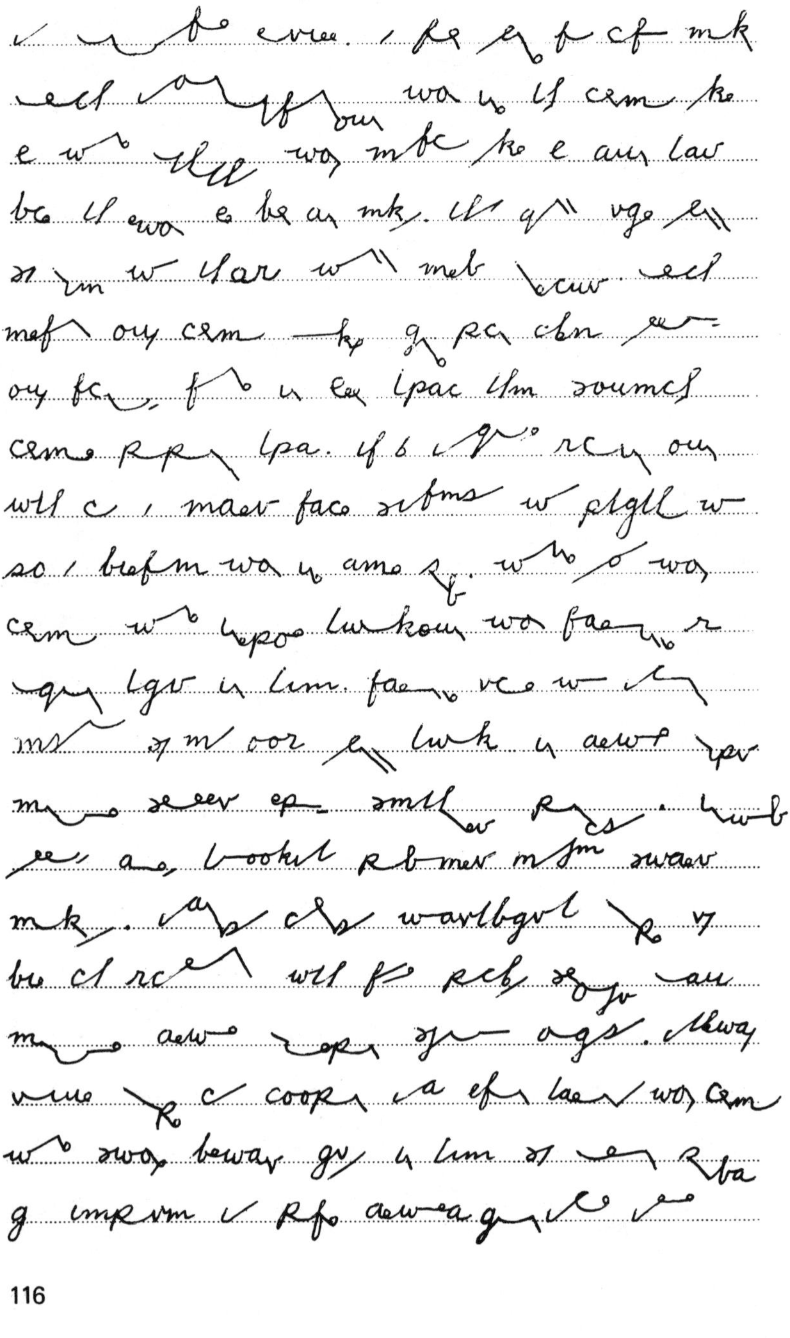

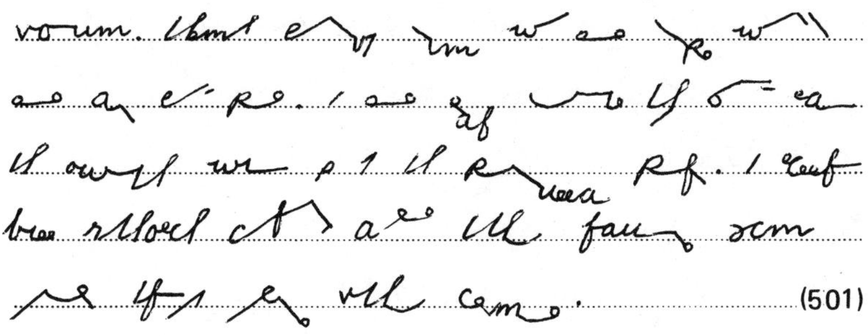

(501)

London Chamber of Commerce

95

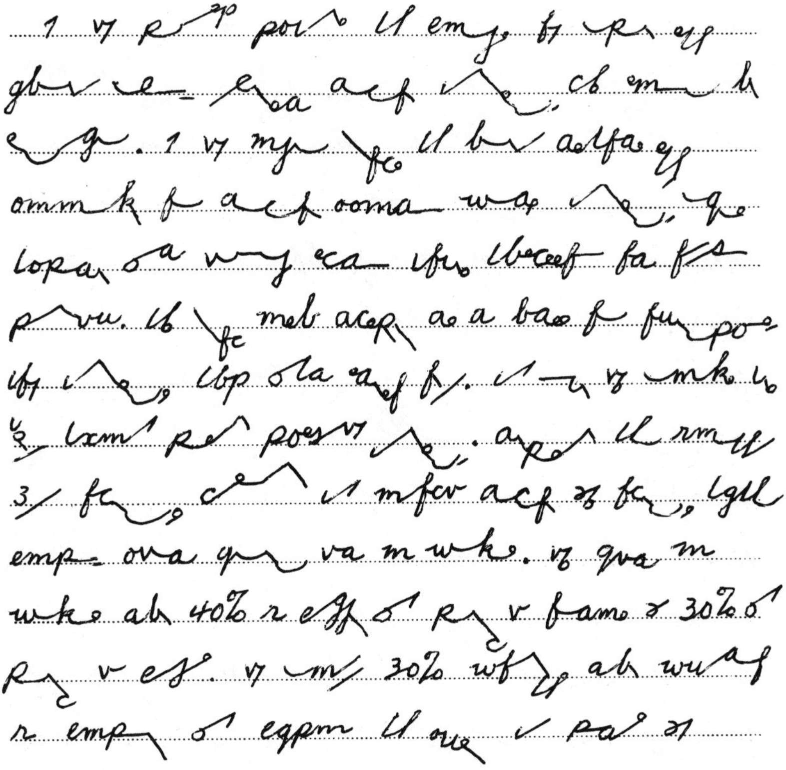

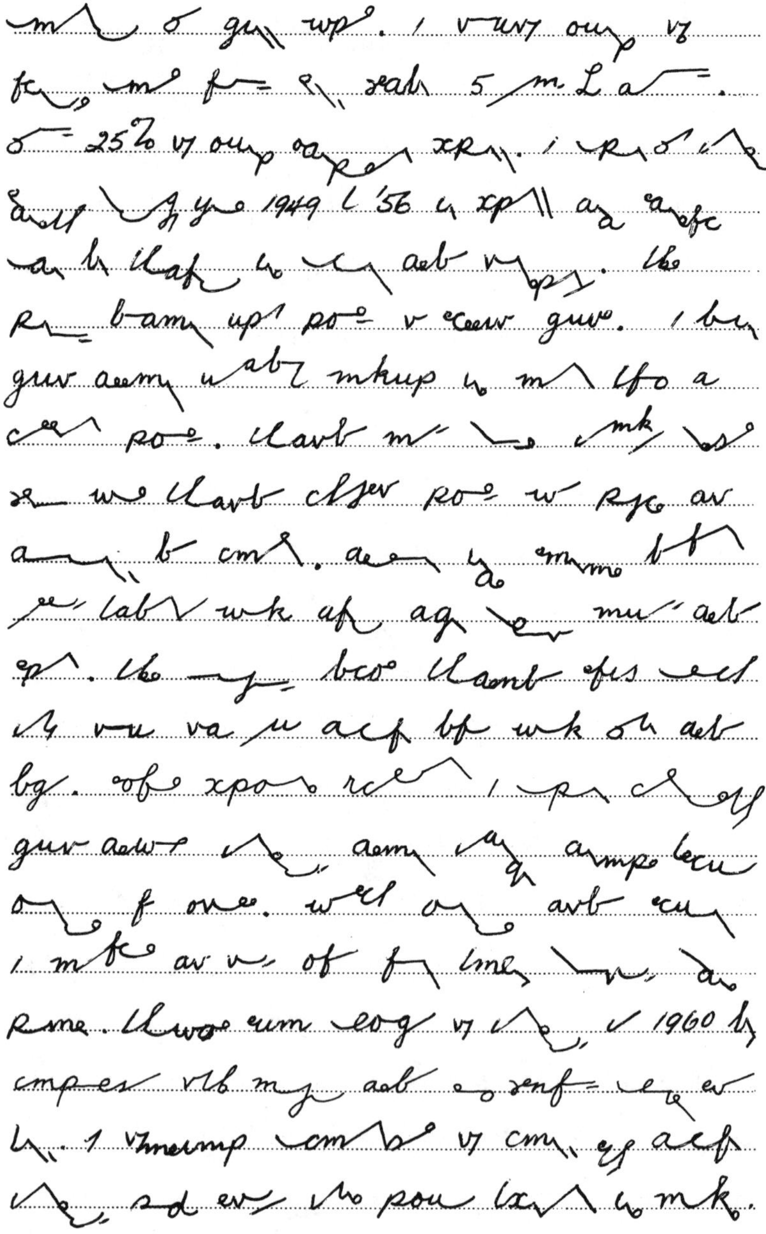

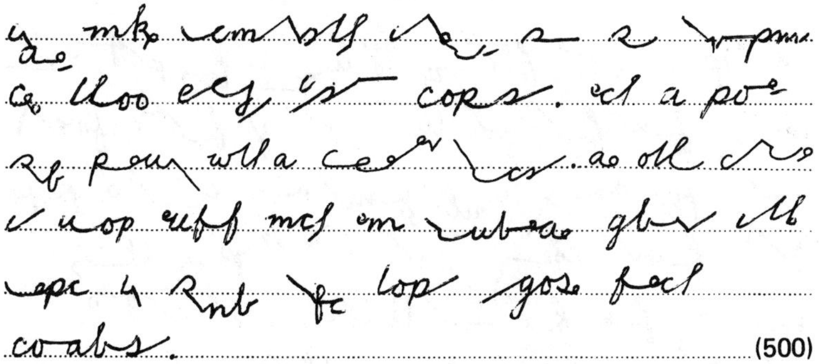

(500)

Pitman Examinations Institute

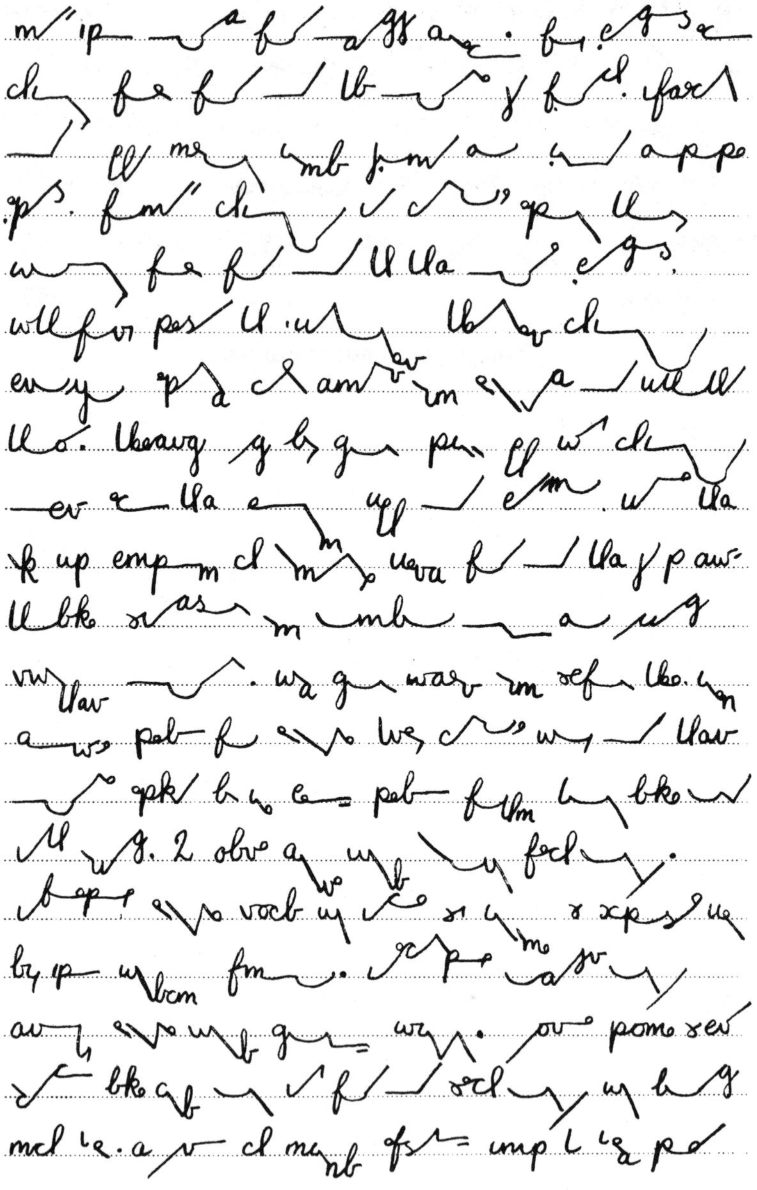

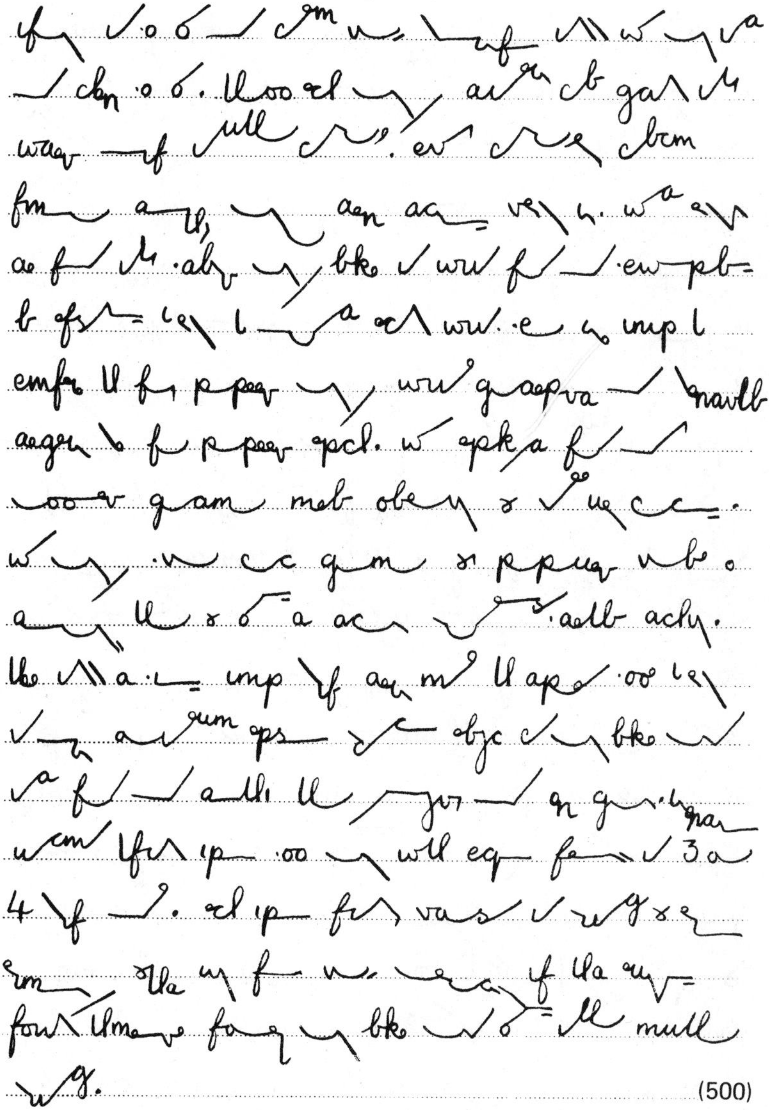

(500)

Pitman Examinations Institute

97

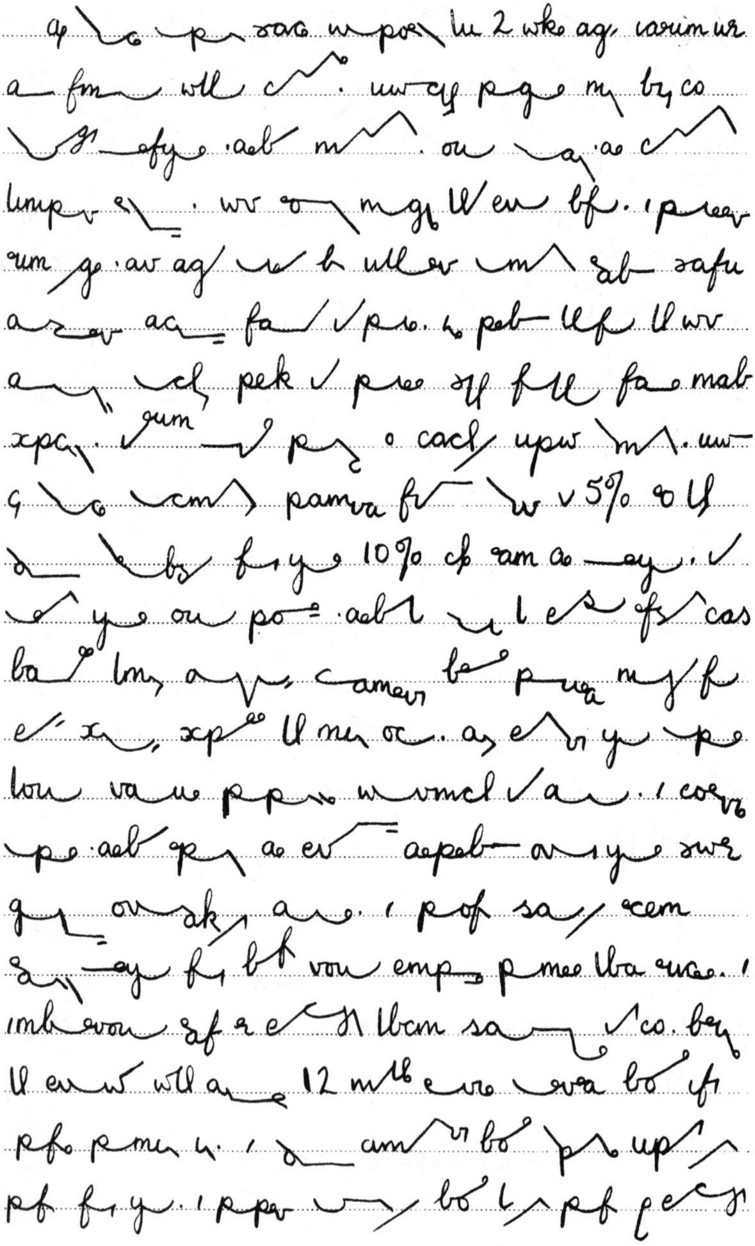

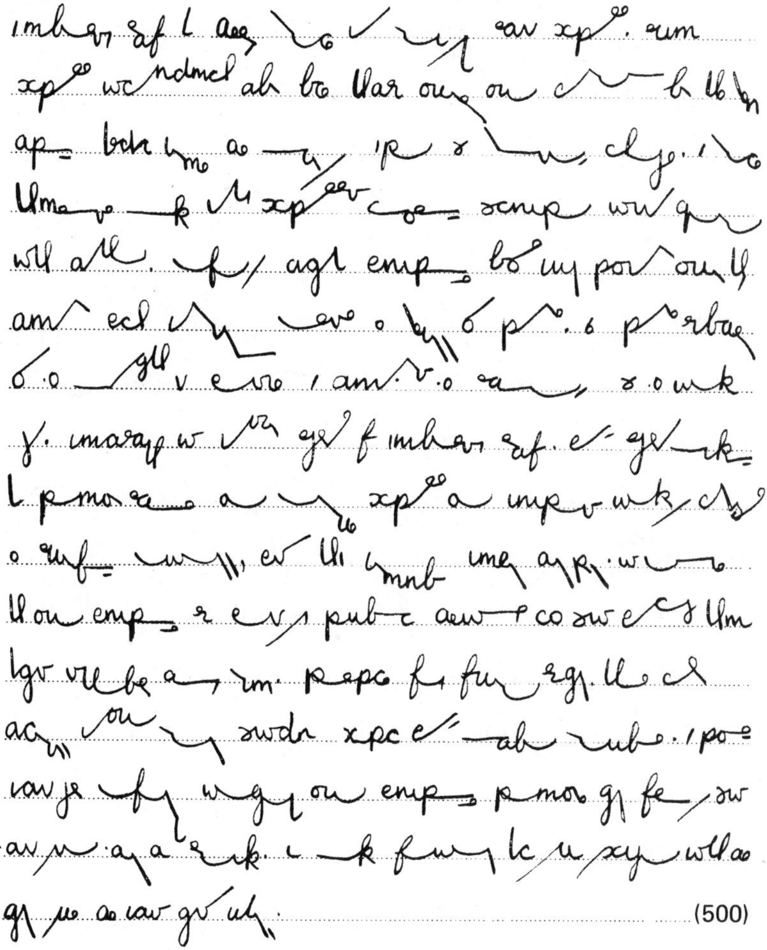

(500)

Pitman Examinations Institute

98

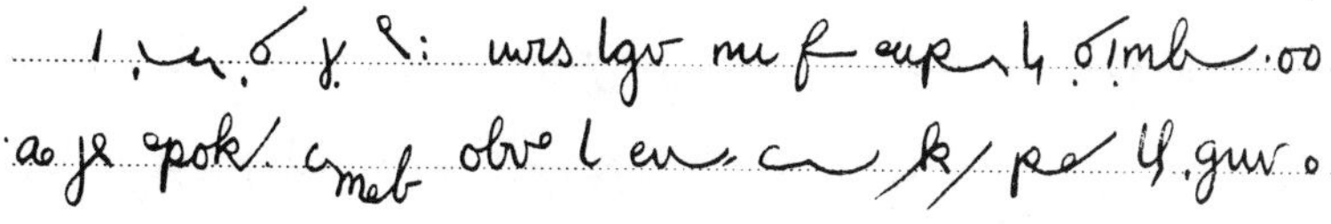

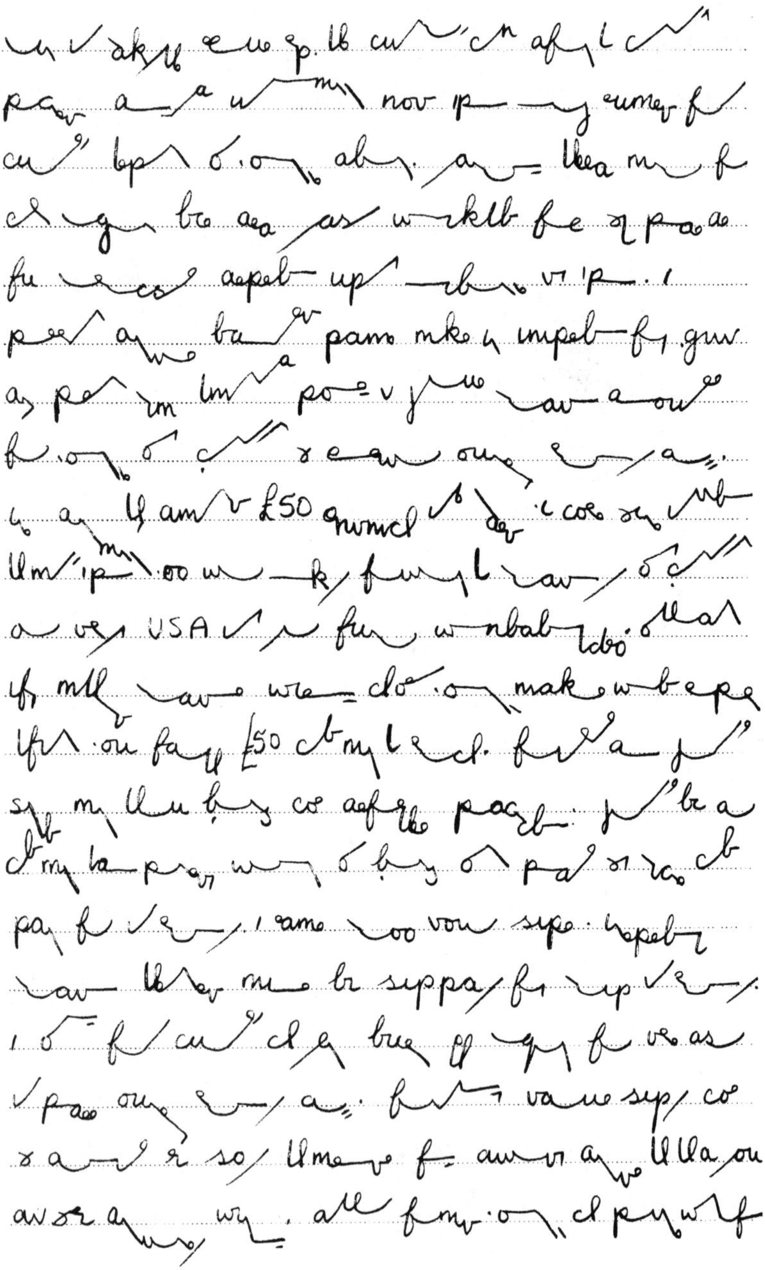

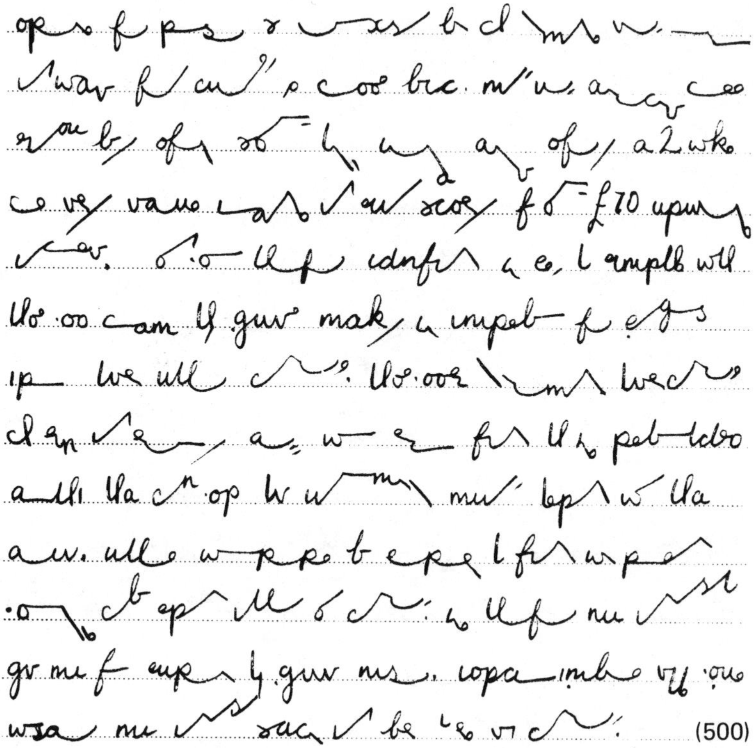

(500)

Pitman Examinations Institute

99

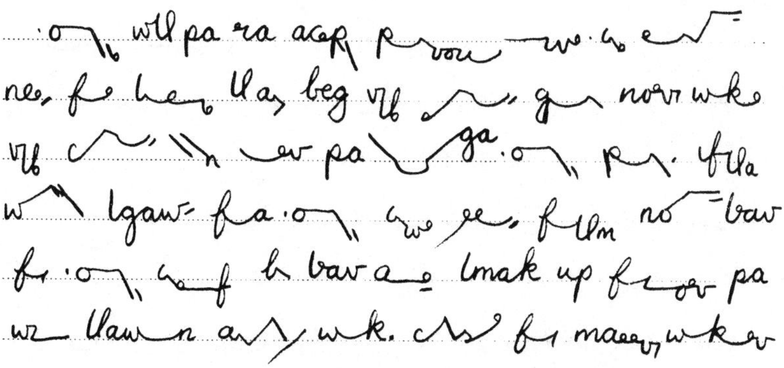

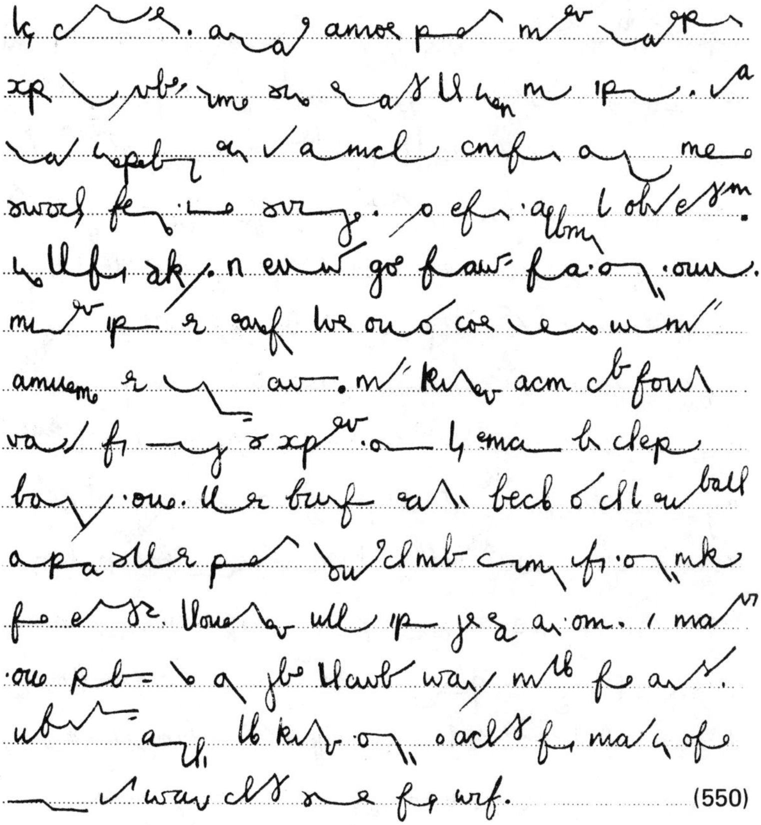

(550)

Pitman Examinations Institute

100

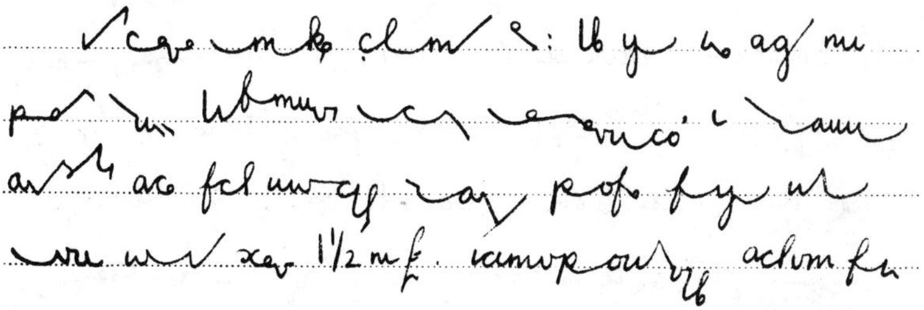

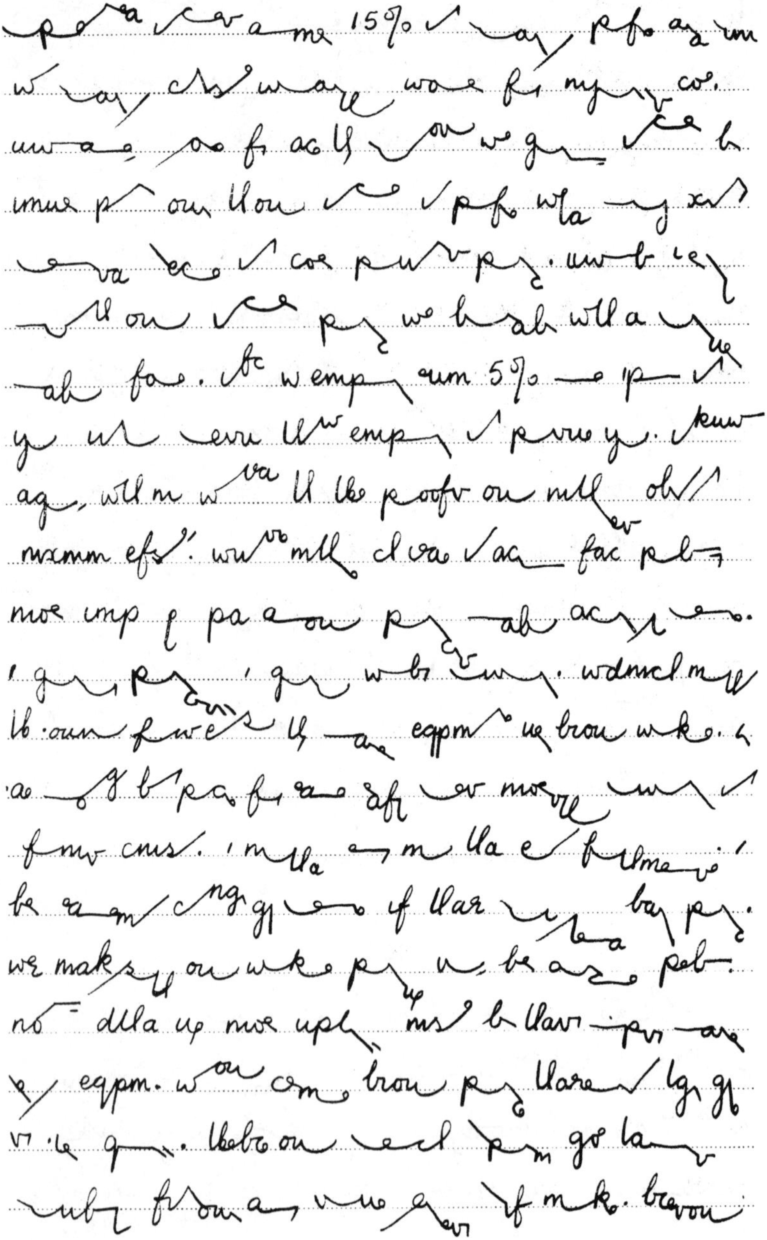

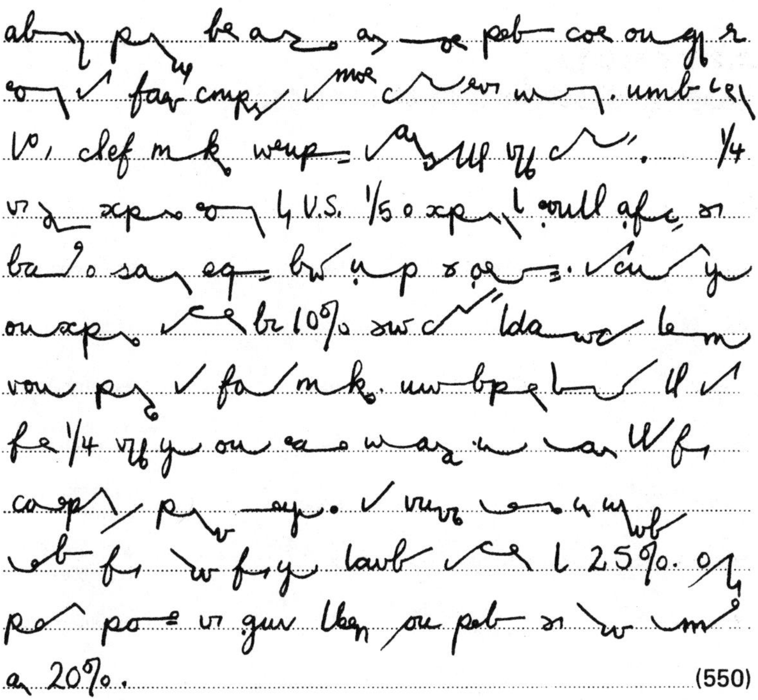

(550)

Pitman Examinations Institute

APPENDIX
SOME SUGGESTED LINKS

A

- absence of our
- after a time
- all in all
- all of us
- amount of which
- and I am glad
- and I shall be pleased
- and in our opinion
- & Sons Limited
- annual general meeting
- as a general rule
- as a result
- as a whole
- as compared with
- as far as possible
- as fully as
- as much as
- as often as possible
- as soon as possible
- as soon as we are
- as we have not
- as we think you may be
- as well as
- as you will have seen
- at the moment
- attention to the

B

- back of this letter
- balance of payments
- balance of trade
- beginning of this month
- best possible
- bills of lading

board of directors

by far the

bring about

by means of

C

copy of the letter

cost of living

D

day to day

dear sir or madam

E

earliest possible moment

F

facts and figures

for some time past

first time

for the first time

for many years

for the present

for me to have a

for the previous year

for several years

for the purpose of

for some time

for the time being

G

general manager

greater part of this

general reserve account

greater than that

H

he must know

hire purchase company

- I am looking forward
- I am pleased to report
- I am very pleased to
- I am very sorry
- I feel sure
- I have no doubt
- I have not been able to
- I have put
- I should like
- I thank you for the
- if required
- if there is no
- in a position
- in accordance
- in addition to
- in fact
- in favour of
- in most cases
- in order to
- in order to make
- in other words
- in regard to the
- in respect of
- in response to your request
- in the circumstances
- in the first instance
- in the first place
- in these circumstances
- in your hands
- in your last letter
- income tax
- informing us
- is a very capable
- it has been a
- it is a matter of
- it is necessary

L

- ladies and gentlemen
- least possible

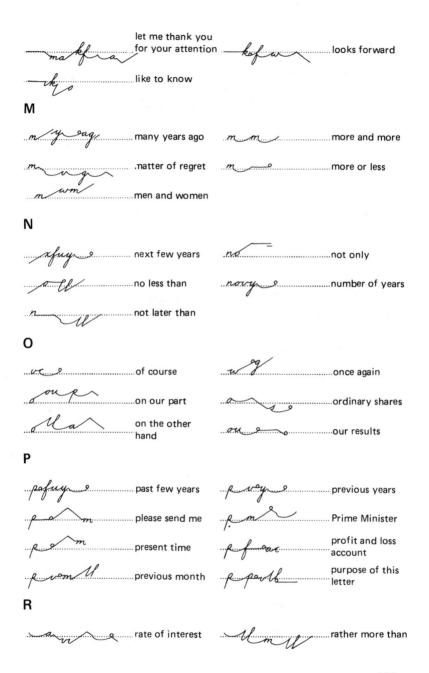

- let me thank you for your attention
- like to know
- looks forward

M

- many years ago
- matter of regret
- men and women
- more and more
- more or less

N

- next few years
- no less than
- not later than
- not only
- number of years

O

- of course
- on our part
- on the other hand
- once again
- ordinary shares
- our results

P

- past few years
- please send me
- present time
- previous month
- previous years
- Prime Minister
- profit and loss account
- purpose of this letter

R

- rate of interest
- rather more than

S

- she must
- she will be
- some time
- such as
- sums of money

T

- takes place
- thank you for your letter
- there has been
- there is nothing
- thinking of you
- this is a matter
- this letter
- those of last year
- to all parts of the
- to do so
- to enter into
- to tell you that
- to send you
- twice a week
- twice a year

U

- up to date

V

- very considerable
- very difficult
- very favourable
- very first time
- very good
- very much
- very soon

W

wrp lbab lof u	we are pleased to be able to offer you the
wavb ab lmak	we have been able to make
wav ak spo	we have taken steps
wav tu f muv	we have to inform you of the
wav tu f mul	we have to inform you that the
wop	we hope
wmexpca	we must expect a
wa kf yl	we thank you for your letter of yesterday
/w av o	we would have no
/w lk	we would like
wa a	wear and tear
w bab lkepa	will be able to keep a
w bp	will be pleased
w glmi	with regard to my
oor	who are

Y

y by	year by year
y u v	year under review
y vj	years of age
udnws	you do not wish
uavgv m	you have given me
u rp	your report
u gr	your request